# Celtic Flame

# Celtic Flame

## The Burden of Patrick

Patrick's *Confession* and *Letter Against the Soldiers of Coroticus,* with *Patrick's Breastplate,* in verse paraphrase with Scripture references, notes, and study guide

T.M. Moore

| Library of Congress Number: | | 00-192010 |
|---|---|---|
| ISBN #: | Hardcover | 0-7388-3535-8 |
| | Softcover | 0-7388-3536-6 |



This book was printed in the United States of America.

**To order additional copies of this book, contact:**
Xlibris Corporation
1-888-7-XLIBRIS
www.Xlibris.com
Orders@Xlibris.com

# CONTENTS

# DEDICATION

For Chuck Colson,
*anamcara*

*As for the saints of God*
*who are in the earth,*
*they are the holy ones in*
*whom is all my delight.*
*Ps. 16.3*

# Abbreviations

Bury J. B. Bury. *The Life of St. Patrick and His Place in History*. New York: Book-of-the-Month Club, 1999.

De Paor Liam De Paor. *Saint Patrick's World*. Notre Dame: University of Notre Dame Press, 1993.

Dumville David N. Dumville, *et al. Saint Patrick A. D. 493-1993*. Woodbridge, UK: The Boydell Press, 1993.

Mackey James P. Mackey, ed. *An Introduction to Celtic Christianity*. Edinburgh: T & T Clark, 1989.

Thompson E. A. Thompson. *Who Was St. Patrick?* New York: St. Martin's Press, 1985.

# Introduction

The patron saint of Ireland is surely one of the most loved and yet least known of all Christian saints. There is hardly a child in Ireland or America—or any other country where the Irish diaspora has reached—who does not know something at least about the patriarch whose day is celebrated every 17 March. Patrick drove the snakes out of Ireland. He bested the high king's druids at Tara in a match of wits and power. He taught the doctrine of the Trinity using a shamrock.

Most such stories have little to do with the historical person of Patrick, being accretions to the legend which began to grow up around him some two centuries after his death. Yet the fact that these stories are told and retold, generation by generation, reveals something about our fascination with this remarkable man, as well as our continuing need for heroes like him.

What we know for certain about Patrick can be briefly summarized: Patrick was born to a Roman official, a nominal Christian, somewhere in the west country of Britain, around the turn of the fifth century. Kidnapped from his well-to-do home by Irish raiders at the age of sixteen, he was taken to Ireland and made to serve as a shepherd for six years. During his period of enslavement he rediscovered his faith in God and, at the prompting of a dream or a vision he believed to have come from God, he escaped, ultimately returning to his home across the Irish Sea. Upon receiving there a vision of the people among whom he had slaved, calling him to come and walk among them once more, he returned to Ireland and prepared for the Gospel ministry, against the wishes of his family and the advice of Church officials. He became a deacon and a priest before ultimately being called as Bishop to the Irish people. His was not the usual sort of bishopric for that period of Church history. Rather than be content with administrative duties and guarding against heresy, Patrick gave himself throughout the entire course of his ministry to the work of evangelizing the pagan Irish, training up men for the priesthood and women as virgins to the Lord, starting new churches, and tending to the spiritual needs of his flocks. Late in life, responding to charges against him from certain superiors in Britain, he recorded what he considered to be the important elements of his calling and ministry in his *Confession*, which, together with the *Letter Against the Soldiers of Coroticus*, are the only extant documents we can be sure to have come from Patrick's own hand. He died somewhere near the middle to end of the fifth century, having faithfully served the Church for over sixty years.

Yet this brief summary does not exhaust the story, for embedded within the pages of these two short documents is a wealth of insights into a truly grand and noble character. Even a cursory reading of these materials yields a picture of a true man of faith, devoted, courageous, single-minded, generous to a fault, imperturbable, and undeviating in his vision and calling, a man whose greatest wish was that he might be honored with a martyr's death, his flesh devoured by animals and his bones scattered by wild birds, so that his legacy might be one solely of glory and honor to God.

Patrick was a man of deep humility, keenly aware of his shortcomings and ever resting on the grace of God to overcome them. Only reluctantly did he finally respond to the charges that were being circulated against him late in life, and then only to his colleagues in ministry in Ireland. He made no grand defense before his detractors in Britain, even though it seems he was being urged to do so. He spoke out boldly, even defiantly, against those who persecuted his flocks; and he expected the people under his care to fall in line with his decisions insofar as they could be shown to be consistent with the teaching of Scripture. He quoted and referred to Scripture lavishly, prayed and fasted constantly, and did whatever was necessary to advance the cause of the Gospel among the people to whom he had been sent. He was, in short, a most remarkable and exemplary servant of God, a most fitting saint and hero for Irish men and women all over the world.

In what follows I have sought to present in a brisk and enjoyable format the burden of Patrick as he recorded it in his own words. Critical editions and scholarly studies of Patrick's life and work are available,[1] as well as excerpts from his writings and biographies composed from the Patrician hagiographies that began to appear in the seventh century.[2] Yet the former are not likely to come into the purview of a general readership, and the latter are either insufficient to represent his burden and character or too clouded with the stuff of legend and myth to be of much use in this vein.

I have chosen to use as the basis for the verse paraphrase which follows Patrick's *Confession* and the *Letter Against the Soldiers of Coroticus*,[3] for these, besides being historically authentic, are the most helpful of the Patrician documents in allowing us to look into—and, hopefully, learn from—the heart of the man. In addition, I have spread in italics throughout the verse paraphrase the stanzas of the hymn, *Patrick's Breastplate*, an eighth-century verse celebrating the faith of the saint.

[1] See, for example, the works cited throughout the narrative.

[2] J. B. Bury's *The Life of St. Patrick and His Place in History*, recently republished by Book-of-the-Month Club (New York: 1999), is the most comprehensive, critical, and respected of these.

[3] As translated from the Latin and given in De Paor. In the verse paraphrase that follows, only the Prologue is original with this author.

While probably not from Patrick's own hand, this hymn seems to me both to capture the essence of his faith and to express the seeds of the Celtic Christian vision which grew out of the impetus provided by Patrick. I have also referred, from time to time, to later Patrician materials, although only to the extent that I found them useful in supporting the central purpose of this book. Where helpful, I have added critical notes to the text, as well as Scripture references designed to illustrate the Biblical foundations of Patrick's burden. I have tried to stay as close as possible to the actual wording of Patrick's texts; for this reason, readers may be disquieted from time to time at an awkward phrase or choice of words, and students of poetry will lament the dearth of poetic devices other than rhyme and meter.

While there is much to learn from Patrick, five lessons in particular stand out from the materials that are paraphrased in what follows. First is Patrick's motivation for service. Patrick pursued his labors amid danger, difficulty, and depravation out of a deep sense of gratitude to God for the grace that had been shown to him. He confessed that he had been an ingrate, justly deserving the wrath of God, when he was carried off into slavery as a boy. Because of his lack of formal schooling, he regarded himself as rustic and unrefined in comparison to his peers in ministry. Thus, he constantly marvels at the grace that was shown to him, both in preserving him through and delivering him from slavery (more than once, by the way) and in using him in the work of the Church. His sense of gratitude to God can be instructive for all, regardless of their callings in life, by reminding us that the "lovingkindness of the Lord is everlasting" toward those on whom He has set His love (Ps. 136).

Second is his piety. Patrick was a deeply spiritual man. He put no confidence in the flesh—in formal training, financial backing, or fancy ministry schemes—but trusted only in God to guide and sustain him day by day. His knowledge of Scripture was exhaustive, and his obedience to it in life and ministry consistent at every turn. He was a man of prayer and faith, humble and self-effacing yet zealous for God and the work to which he had been called. In a time when true piety seems to be on the wane, we can learn from Patrick how such a life can bring meaning and strength to all one's pursuits.

Third, Patrick was consumed by the desire to win lost men and women to faith in Christ. Convinced that the last days were upon him, he seems to have had no permanent base of ministry—the claims of Armagh notwithstanding—but itinerated throughout much of Ireland, preaching, evangelizing, making disciples, and caring for his flocks wherever he went. He would not allow his work to be impeded by jealous local rulers, postponed by Church officials, or interrupted in order to go to Britain to make a defense of his ministry. He steadfastly and courageously refused simply to sit by when ruthless wolves in sheep's clothing ravaged his flocks. His Gospel and preaching were completely orthodox, and he bore down on those who heard him with untiring calls for repentance and faith. He feared no man, but God alone, and lived to make Him known. In our day, when zeal for the work of evangelism has begun to flag and a Gospel of self-indulgence is becoming more and more the creed of many in the Church, we can benefit greatly from the example of the Gospel flame that burned in the heart of Patrick.

Fourth, Patrick's courage and conviction stand as examples for us today. He overcame lack of education and familial support, opposition from peers (on three occasions), the dangers of a wild and uncivilized land, unremitting material depravation, and temptations on every hand to persevere in a calling that he believed had come to him from God. As a sidelight to this aspect of Patrick's burden, he also presents us with something of a study in the fallibility of Church courts. His initial going to Ireland was questioned by those in authority over him. His advancement to the office of bishop was held up by his superiors over a trifling matter (although he later acknowledged that, at the time, he was not ready for the office). And his superiors sought to remove him from the field on charges that were palpably false, as anyone in Ireland could have testified. None of this daunted Patrick or deterred him from what he knew God had called him to do. We can learn from him how, in the face of discouragement and distractions, to keep our eyes on the Lord as we go forth to serve Him each day.

Finally, Patrick's life is a study in loving the unlovely. Ireland in Patrick's day was considered the ends of the earth. So fierce, wild, and uncivilized were the Irish people that the Romans never mounted an effort to subdue them. They were a people devoted to tribe and tradition, and would go to war with anyone who brought offense against their family or trespassed on their lands. Their communal organization was unlike anything in civilized Rome, and, though not lacking in a distinct culture, they knew neither writing nor formal education until after Patrick's arrival. Yet Patrick knew the Irish people at first-hand, having been a slave among them for six years, and he loved them passionately, courageously, and sacrificially. If more of this kind of love could be found among the spiritual descendants of Patrick today, it is not difficult to imagine the difference it could make in the inner cities and underdeveloped nations of the world, or among the poor, outcast, and diseased of society.

My hope is that readers will find this narrative of Patrick's burden entertaining and informative, yet not merely so. I have chosen to prepare the verse paraphrase in heroic couplets, both because it makes the narrative eminently readable and because I find it a fitting form for the retelling of the burden of this heroic saint. The study guide that accompanies the text is designed to help readers delve more deeply into the

Christian roots and lessons that may be gained from an understanding of Patrick's burden.

Many people have had a hand in helping to make this study possible. I should like to thank Dr. and Mrs. Lane Adams, my parents-in-law, as well as the many others who have encouraged me along the way, in particular, Brian and Phyllis Bankard. Most especially, I am grateful for my wife, Susie, for her strength, support, keen insights, encouragement, and unflagging faith. May He Who called Patrick and used him so abundantly in the work of His Church be pleased to use this humble offering to rekindle something of that saint's burden among his spiritual kindred in our generation.

*Soli Deo Gloria*
T. M. Moore
Philippi, WV

# Prologue

Throughout the crumbling empire, as the light
of glory fast was fading and a night
of barbarism, bleak and bitter, fell
on every land, it must have seemed that hell
itself had vomited its unwashed hosts
Rev. 9.1-11 upon the earth to stifle Roman boasts
of eternality, and bring a reign
of pillage, plunder, punishment, and pain
upon a once-proud people. Even Rome
itself did not escape, where every home
was looted, burned, or stricken by the sword.[4]
To some, it was the judgment of the Lord
against a vain, corrupt, decaying way
of life.[5] The time had come for Rome to pay
the piper, for the end was near, when from
His throne, the Lord in judgment fierce would come
to save His own and settle the affairs
Mt. 13.36-43 of men, or so it seemed. The wheat and tares
would soon be gathered up, and so that none
may have excuse before His judgment throne,

[4] After a century of harassment and invasion by barbarian armies from north of the Rhine River, Rome fell in 410, an event which sent shock waves of fear and dread throughout the Roman Empire.

[5] This, for example, was the opinion of Augustine, who wrote *The City of God* to respond to critics who were claiming that Rome had fallen because it had forsaken the ancient gods for the Christian faith.

a man was sent where never cleric's sole
had trod—to Ireland, to the very hole
and pit of paganism, which had scoffed
at Roman civilizing power and doffed
its hat to naught but blood—to feed the few
among them who confessed the Lord, and do
whatever could be done to win the rest.[6]
Palladius was this cleric's name, and blessed
by Pope Celestine, he to Ireland came
to serve the Church and propagate the Name
Jn. 9.4; of Jesus while it yet was day. He made
1 Thess. 5.8-11 a start,[7] but as the day began to fade
against the growing darkness all throughout
the Roman world and nations round about,
there in the land of Celts and druids, the light
of goodness flickered frail against the night.
A bold and faithful handful made their stand
amid the pagans in that cold, hard land

[6] Ireland had never come under Roman authority. It was a wild and, in many ways, uncivilized land, governed by local kings and organized according to tribes in a loose confederation characterized by an agrarian society of close-knit family groups, inter-tribal warfare, druidical religion, and pagan myth. When Palladius was sent to be the first bishop of the Irish, only a handful of believers, mostly slaves captured from Christian lands, lived scattered throughout the island. See Bury, chapter IV, for an excellent introduction to Ireland in Patrick's day.

[7] Palladius was sent by Pope Celestine in 431. There are no certain records concerning the success of his ministry, and in recent years a measure of controversy has swirled around the role of Palladius in Irish Church history (cf. Dumville, 65–88). A contemporary of Palladius remarks that some progress of the Gospel seems to have been realized among the Irish during the years of his episcopate (Thompson, 170–175). It is not impossible, and perhaps likely, that Patrick's initial preparation for ministry was under his tutelage or that of his immediate successors.

of wild indifference.[8] Yet a candle glowed
within that night,[9] the light of one who owed
his life to God and to His Son, and he
became a flame that burned so brilliantly
that it would turn the night to glorious day,
and show the world the everlasting Way.

---

[8] Muirchu, writing in the seventh century, describes the Irish of Palladius' day as "wild and obdurate" (De Paor, 179).

[9] I am following Thompson, who believes that, shortly after his "Macedonian vision," Patrick went to Ireland, where he received his initial training and began his ministry, even before he was consecrated as a bishop (38).

# 1. A Most Uncultivated Man

My name is Patrick, and for sixty years[10]
I have, with many labors, joys, and tears,
proclaimed the Name of Jesus in these parts,
although I know within my heart of hearts
I am a most uncultivated man,[11]
1 Tim. 1.15 — the least of all the faithful in this land,
2 Cor. 10.10 — and looked upon with scorn by many. I
have sought with all my strength the Lord on high
to serve, not seeking status, wealth, or fame,
but just the celebration of the Name
Eph. 2.1-5 — of Him Who looked on me with mercy when
I was an ingrate, and the slave of men.
It is with great reluctance and regret
that I must offer my defense and set
aside the greater work to which the Lord
has called me, that I might address some word

[10] The actual dates of Patrick's ministry can only be approximately known. Traditionally, scholars have assigned a date of 432 to the beginning of his ministry, with an outside date of ca. 490 as his death. See De Paor, 5–7; Dumville, 39–43; Hanson, in Mackey, 27, 28; and Thompson, 166–175. In declaring his ministry to have been sixty years in length, Patrick may be including everything from his initial period of training to the time of his writing.

[11] This is a self-conscious shortcoming that he will later explain and return to many times.

of vindication for my ministry.[12]
But there are those who seek to challenge me,
who, for my rudeness, my simplicity,
or youthful folly, would discredit me
and leave these many flocks whom God has put
into my care without a shepherd. What
am I to do, except to state my case
and offer my confession to the face
Gal. 1.10 of God and men? The Lord will hear and judge
these words, which I offer without spite or grudge,
and will approve the work that I have done[13]
and guard the souls who have for Him been won.

*I call this day to shield and shelter me*
*a mighty power, the Holy Trinity!*
*His threeness I affirm; His oneness I*
*confess, Who made of nothing earth and sky*
*and all that is within them through His love,*
*and rules creation from His throne above!*

Calpornius, my father, son of the late
Potitus, was a deacon. His estate
was near to Banna Venta Berniae,[14]

[12] Patrick's ministry was apparently being questioned by superiors in Britain, who seem to have charged him with pecuniary motives in his ministry. After building a case for the validity of his call, he will address this charge directly in section V.

[13] Thompson takes issue with Patrick over his failure to mention any of his predecessors or colleagues throughout the course of his *Confession* (148–150). However, given that it was Patrick himself who was being challenged, it seems natural that he would focus in his apologetic on his own work and his calling from the Lord, and that he would be careful not to say anything that might be construed as laying blame on his teachers (for example, for his many shortcomings) or wanting to include his colleagues in his alleged guilt.

where, as a priest, his father served to say
the liturgy and guard the flock of God.
When I was sixteen years of age, the rod
of judgment fell on me, as I deserved,
and I was carried off and made to serve
in Ireland, as were many others. We
had turned our backs on God impiously,
and scorned His Law, refusing to obey
Acts 2.38-40 our bishops who proclaimed to us the way
of God's salvation and exhorted us
to put aside our sinful ways and trust
the Lord. Yet we refused to know our good
and loving Savior, as we clearly should;
Rom. 1.18-32 and so he showed Himself to us in wrath.
He fell upon us as we walked the path
of wickedness, and scattered us among
so many foreign peoples; we were flung
out to the ends of the earth, where to this day,
appropriately, I make my humble way
among a foreign people.

But the Lord
did not forsake me there, and by His Word
revealed my unbelief,[15] so that I might,
however late, set my offenses right
Mt. 22.37, 38 and turn to Him with all my heart. For He,
though I was nothing, yet regarded me,
1 Tim. 1.12, 13 and pitied both my ignorance and youth.
Ps. 71.6 He cared for me before I knew the truth
or could discern the evil from the good.

[14] The exact place of Patrick's home in Britain is uncertain, although it was doubtless somewhere in the west country (Dark, in Dumville, 19–24).

[15] His suffering and loneliness led him to reflect on the faith he was instructed in as a child and to turn to the Lord in prayer, as he will show.

He comforted me as a father would
his son, and guarded me throughout my years
of foolishness and sin. And so, with tears
of gratitude, I must proclaim the great
and many blessings which the Lord of late
has granted me, here in the land of my
2 Cor. 5.11-15 captivity. For this is how I try
to make repayment for the way the Lord
revealed to me His glory and His Word
through capture and enslavement: I declare
His wonders to the races everywhere
Dt. 6.4; Dt. 4.39 beneath the heavens. [16]For there is but one
eternal God; no other has begun
to be, or ever shall. He is without
Eph. 3.14, 15 beginning, God the Father, He about
Whom I must sing. And all that is began
Ps. 104 to be from Him; He governs earth and man
and everything that is, as we are taught.
Jn. 3.16 His Son is Jesus Christ, the One Who bought
us with His blood. We testify that He
Jn. 1.1, 2 was with the Father in eternity,
and was by Him begotten in a way
that cannot be described. All that today
Jn. 1.3 we see—and even that which eyes cannot
behold—was made by Him. And so we ought
Phil. 2.5-7 to worship Him, Who for our sakes became

[16] Note Patrick's orthodoxy in this brief declaration of his faith, lines 121–156. In the seventh and eighth centuries, and occasionally yet today, Celtic Christians have been accused of courting Pelagianism. While it is true that this early fifth-century heresy arose in Britain and made re-appearance in Celtic lands from time to time, I am not persuaded that the Celtic fathers or their followers were anything other than as orthodox as Patrick.

1 Cor. 15.20-26 a Man, demolished death, received a Name
Eph. 1.20, 21 above all others, and was taken to
His heavenly home and to His Father, Who
Mt. 28.18 awarded Him all power in earth and heaven.
Eph. 1.22 For everything to Jesus has been given,
Phil. 2.8-11 that every knee should bow and every tongue
confess, of things on earth and things among
the dead and in the heavens, that He is Lord
and God, and they should all obey His Word.
Acts 16.31 And we believe in Him and long to see
Rev. 22.20 the day of His return, for it will be
Jn. 5.22-29 upon us soon. Then He shall judge the dead
and all who live, and will, as He has said,
return to all according to what they
have done, and usher in eternal day.
Acts 2.32, 33 He poured upon us so abundantly
Eph. 1.13, 14 His Holy Spirit, a gift and pledge, that we
should immortality possess. And all
Rom. 10.9-13 who trust in Him and on His mercy call
Jn. 1.12 He makes the sons of God, and with Him, heirs
of everlasting bliss. So we declare,
confess, and love Him as one God within
the Trinity, that Holy Name. Through Him
Ps. 50.15 the prophet Asaph said, "Now call on Me
when trouble comes, and I will set you free,
and you shall glorify My Name." Again
Tobit 12.7 He says, "It is an honorable thing that men
should celebrate God's works and all proclaim
the glory of His holy, matchless Name."

Although I am a most imperfect man
in many ways, please try to understand
my motives, and to know what sort of man
I am, especially you who take your stand
with me or are my kin.[17] I know the cost

of lying, as the Lord has said, "You must
Ps. 5.6 destroy the liar," and again, "The tongue
Wisdom 1.11 that lies destroys the soul." And then among
His teachings in the Gospel, "The idle word
Mt. 12.36 that people speak, they shall before the Lord
give an account for it." And so I know
that I must be in greatest dread, in so
much fear and trembling should I herein lie,
that when I stand before the Lord on high
I shall incur His wrath. For on that day
Rev. 6.12-17 no man can hide himself or sneak away
from His all-searching eye; and every one
2 Cor. 5.10 of us must justify what we have done
here in the flesh before His holy face,
and He will not forget and not erase
the smallest sin. And so I know that I
Mt. 5.33-37 must speak the truth herein, and must not lie.[18]

Indeed, for quite some time I have had in mind
to state my case, but feared, lest you should find
my lack of education reason to
condemn me. Unlike many others, who

---

[17] Patrick's *Confession* seems to have had three audiences in mind, all of them Britons (as Thompson has persuasively shown, 115–124). First, there were his colleagues in ministry. They had heard the charges against him, no doubt for many years, and were being reminded of his conduct in ministry and could reflect on the truth of what he said. Second were his kin, by which he probably intends any other Britons living in Ireland or perhaps relatives back in Britain who may also have heard the charges against him. Finally, and only indirectly, are his accusers, whom he addresses as "professors" or "reverend doctors," as I have rendered it.

[18] Patrick virtually swears an oath of death on himself if he should lie. His account is certainly among the most straightforward and unadorned of Celtic Christian literature.

absorbed in full both Scripture and the ways
of men[19] throughout their lives, and spent their days
perfecting language and its use in their
own native tongue, I must with greatest care—
but not, alas, with skill—my words translate
from Irish, which has been my tongue of late,
into that language which I have not used
since youth.[20] So if I seem at times confused
or ungrammatical, then you will know
my erudition[21] and why I was so
delayed in making my defense. For I
am not unmindful, as it says, "For by
Eccl. 10.12 his language is the wise man known," as will
sound judgment, knowledge, and all truth be. Still,
excuses, be they ever true, will not
persuade, especially if we take the lot
of them together with the vanity
of my presumption, as old age to me
has come, of thinking that I might achieve
more than I could when I was young.[22] I grieve
when I recall it was my sins that cut
my education short, for I was put
into the bonds of slavery, as I said,
because of my rebellious ways. Instead
of keeping books and lectures, I was made
to shepherd in a foreign land, afraid,
alone, and far from home. But who believes

[19] Literally, "the law."

[20] That is, Latin, which Patrick had known as a boy, but which he had only infrequently used among the Irish whom he served. Patrician scholars uniformly testify as to the rusticity and crudeness of Patrick's Latin.

[21] He means his lack of erudition.

[22] He means here skill in use of the Latin language.

me, even as I say again how thieves
from Ireland took me captive when I was
a beardless boy, before I knew the laws
of God and men? And so I am ashamed
today, and fearful I will be defamed
for laying bear my lack of learning. For
I lack the fluency to say it more
concisely or expressively, although
my spirit longs to do so. Yet I know
that I will try with all my soul and heart
to state my burden, though I lack the art
you might expect. And if I did possess
the verbal skills with which most men are blessed
who hold this post, yet I would not refrain
from speaking, thankful for what I have gained
from God. And if perhaps I seem to some
to vaunt myself, yet it is given from
Is. 32.4[23] the mouth of God, "The stammering tongue will learn
to speak of peace."

How much more ought we yearn
for this, since it is written, "we to you
2 Cor. 3.2, 3 are letters of salvation, even to
the end of earth." And though my language flow
uneasily, all blocked and turgid, know
that "it is written on your hearts not by
mere ink, but by the Spirit of God on high."
For even rustic backwardness has been
created by the one Who made all men.

---

[23] De Paor's comment here is useful. He cites this reference then adds by way of explanation, "with the coming of the righteous kingdom – a hint of Patrick's millenarian view of his mission" (302).

So, in the first place, I an exile am,
a plainly rustic and unlearned man,
who knows not how he should provide for his
own future. At the same time, I of this
one thing am certain: I was once abased,
just like a fallen stone, or one that's placed
into deep mire. And He Who is mighty came
and through the goodness of His gracious Name
has lifted me to set me high upon
Ps. 40.1-4 the wall. Because of this I raise my song
and ought to shout aloud, to thank and praise
the Lord for all His blessings, all the ways
He cares for me both here and in the age
Ps. 106.2 to come, so many that the wisest sage
could not begin to comprehend them all.
So be astonished, all of you, the small
and great alike, who fear the Lord. And you,
most reverend doctors, listen closely to
my words, and pay attention. Who raised me—
yes, stupid me—unto this ministry,
from out of those who seemed to be so wise
and skilled in rhetoric and law?[24] Whose eyes
with favor looked on me and burdened and
prepared me for my mission to this land,

[24] Patrick is recalling the ecclesiastical procedure by which he was chosen as bishop. He was not appointed by the pope, popular tradition notwithstanding; rather, he was appointed by bishops in Britain and was accountable to them for his ministry. Initially he had been rejected for the post, but continued his training in Ireland, ultimately becoming a deacon before being ordained a priest and, finally, appointed bishop over the Irish. He is recalling the fact that his superiors chose him for this post over a group of better-educated candidates, no doubt because of his zeal, sense of calling, progress in Scripture, and knowledge of the Irish people and language.

and brought me here to be of service to
this people, in humility and truth?

And so, I take it as a measure of
my faith in God and in His Triune love
that, not regarding danger, I made known
God's gift and the eternal peace His own
may have as He provides; and that I spread
His Name throughout this land, from foot to head,
both dutifully and without fear. And thus
I have a legacy of those who trust
the Lord—so many thousands of my sons
and brothers—whom by laboring I have won
to Him and baptized in His holy Name.
This is my burden, and my only claim.

# 2. Holy Servant Boy

*This day to shield me I will call upon*
*the power of Christ, the power which has begun*
*among us with His coming to the lost*
*and His baptism; power which on the cross*
*was shown as He was dying for our sins;*
*the power which, with His rising up, begins*
*the Kingdom age; the power by which He went*
*again to heaven, from which He had been sent;*
*His power I call upon which in the end*
*will bring Him back in judgment over men.*

So I was not a fit or worthy man
for what the Lord has granted me; I am
a minor servant in His Kingdom. And
I am amazed that, having at His hand
endured calamities and burdens great,
and having suffered in the humble state
of slavery, now, after all these years,
I weep with humble and rejoicing tears
Eph. 3.20, 21 to see what God has done, much more than I
had thought or hoped to see before I die.

But after I to Ireland came I found
myself a slave, and pastured sheep around
the hills and meadows in the west. You can
imagine my despair, my sorrow, and
my loneliness, a boy of sixteen years.

My days were filled with toil, my nights with fears.
Phil. 4.6, 7 And so I turned to prayer to find relief
in God, although I had not made belief
my firm conviction as of yet.[25] I prayed
throughout the day, and many times I stayed
awake, beseeching God to pity me.
I found the love and fear of God to be
advancing in my soul; my faith began
to grow, and I began to understand
Phil. 2.12, 13 that God was working in my spirit. I
Ps. 55.16, 17 would pray a hundred times each day, and by
the light of moon and stars, as often, too.
I found through prayer a pleasant means to do
my work without complaint or fear, and would
remain out on the mountain and in the woods
through snow or frost or rain. I rose to pray
Mk. 1.35 before the morning light appeared each day,
and suffered no adversity, nor was
I sluggish in my work. It was because
the Spirit of the living God was in
me seething, freeing me from fear and sin.

And it was there, while I was tending sheep,
I was alone one night, and fast asleep,
when, in a dream, I heard a voice that said
Acts 13.1-3 to me, "Your fast[26] is good, there on your bed

[25] Notice Patrick's honest admission that, although he was given much to prayer, he was not yet a true believer. He would only come to faith a little later, and that, no doubt, as an answer to his many prayers.

[26] Patrick alludes to his practice of fasting, which was apparently so much an ordinary part of his growing spiritual discipline that he did not feel it was necessary even to mention it along with his prayers. The assumption seems to be that the readers of his *Confession* would understand that fasting and prayer went together.

among the flocks, for soon you will return
to your own land." My heart began to burn
with wonder at this word. Then later on
that night this strange pronouncement came: "Be gone!
Behold, your ship is ready." Could it be?
Then shortly afterwards I rose to flee
from him whose flocks I had for six long years[27]
been keeping. Yet my vessel was not near
but as it happened, it was more than two
hundred long miles away. And yet I knew
no person in that place, nor ever there
Phil. 4.19 had been before. With only God to care
for me, I fled, and made my way by night
across this land, while keeping out of sight
of men and making do as best I could.

And so it came to pass that in the good
and gracious will of God, Who guided me,
and without fear, I finally reached the sea,
and there I saw a ship. And on the day
that I arrived, that ship its anchor weighed,
as though it had been meant for me. So I
explained that I had means to pay for my
conveyance, yet I would not, for the fear
Ps. 16.4 of God, agree to suck their nipples.[28] Here
I met with disappointment, though it was
my hope that certain of these men, because

[27] Patrick is now 22 years old.

[28] This practice, which strikes us as bizarre, was apparently some pagan rite of submission. It may have been adopted by some Celtic Christians at a later period, although not with universal approval. For a fictional account of its use, see the Celtic novel, *Sun Dancing*, by Geoffrey Moorhouse (New York: Harcourt Brace & Company, 1997), pp. 47, 48.



8-MOOR

they all were pagans, might begin to know
the Lord because of me.[29] "Your wish to go
with us is futile," said the captain in
a sharp and angry voice, to my chagrin.
I turned away on hearing this, to go
back to the shelter where I lodged. And so
I prayed to God, "O Lord, why have I come
so many miles, to be rejected from
this vessel?" Yet before my prayer was done
I was accosted by the voice of one
of them, who shouted loudly after me,
"The men are calling you; come speedily
and get aboard." So I returned to them
immediately, and then began the men
to say to me, "We will accept you in
good faith, so bind yourself in friendship then
with us by any way you wish." And so
because of this,[30] the captain let me go
with them, and we set sail at once.

For three
full days our vessel sailed across the sea
until at last we reached the land.[31] Throughout

---

[29] Already Patrick's evangelistic zeal is beginning to be in evidence.

[30] Apparently the sailors reasoned with the captain and persuaded him to change his mind. We do not know what convinced him, but, as Thomspon suggests (27–29) they may have been planning to sell him into slavery upon reaching their destination.

[31] Probably Gaul (France). It would not have taken three days to arrive in Britain, nor would they have been likely to wander there for many days without seeing anyone (lines 415 ff.). Further, it should not have taken "years" for Patrick to reach his home upon once arriving in Britain (lines 473–76). Thompson shows convincingly that the journey to Gaul from Ireland could easily have been made in three days, and this is the most likely place

Acts 1.8 our journey, I would tell the men about
the Lord, and urge them to repent. I said,[32]
Ps. 50.21 "Our God is not as you suppose; instead,
Ps. 22.28 He is the God of every man, the Lord
Jn. 1.1-3 of earth and heaven, Who by His holy Word
has made the sea and rivers, and the sun
and moon and stars. He fashioned every one
Heb. 1.3 of them, and keeps them in their place. And He
Ps. 104 is Lord of all the mountains, every tree
and creature, and the verdant valleys. He
is God in heaven, and dwells within the sea
and on the earth and underneath the sky.
His life is in all things; all things are by
Acts 17.26-28 His grace created and sustained. He makes
them all to live, and rules without mistake
or error. He the light of sun each day
rekindles, and the light which guides your way
by night—the moon and stars—He builds for you
because He is a gracious God, and true.
He gives us wells in arid land, and dry
and welcome islands in the sea, all by
Ps. 2; Jn. 3.16 His grace and goodness. And He has a Son,
Who is with Him eternal, and of One
essential being. He is not younger than
the Father, as, of course, it is with man,

---

referred to at this point (23, 24). Patrick will later on express a desire to go to Gaul, which could have expressed, as with his enslavement in Ireland, a desire to minister in the land in which he was formerly a slave.

[32] This sample of Patrick's witness is inserted here from *Bishop Tirechan's Account of Patrick's Journey*, a seventh-century life of the saint (De Paor, 163, 164). I have chosen to insert this here because, while its theology is doubtless more sophisticated than Patrick's understanding at this time would have allowed, it has a note of authenticity about it and it seems particularly relevant to the context.

nor is the Father younger than the Son.
Mt. 28.19 But with the Spirit they are Three in One,
together from eternity, without
the slightest separation." Thus about
Acts 2.40 such things I often spoke, and urged the men
to trust in Him.

And so it happened, when
we had for many days[33] been walking through
a wilderness, the men ran out of food,
and they grew weak from hunger. Then to me
the captain spoke, "You claim your God to be
all powerful and great. Why can't you pray
to Him for us? For as it is, today
we will from hunger perish, and we do
not hope to see another human who
can meet our need." With confidence I said
to him, "Believe in God. He'll give you bread
Acts 14.17 to fill your stomachs. Turn to Him with all
your hearts, since nothing is too great or small
for Him. Believe that He can meet your need
today, for He has plenteous gifts to feed
and care for you." Then, with God's help, it came
about, and to the glory of His Name,
a herd of pigs appeared before our eyes.
They killed and ate their fill, and on that wise
continued for two nights, until their strength
was once again renewed and they at length
were able to continue. For along
the way some had dropped out; they were not strong
enough to carry on, and were half-dead,
but were recovered. So to God our Head
Jms. 1.17 and our Provider I gave thanks and praise,

[33] Patrick actually says twenty-eight days, here and in line 436.

Who cared for us throughout the many days
we wandered in that land. And from that day
I gained prestige among the men. When they
some honey found, they offered some to me
and said, "This is a sacrifice that we
have offered to our gods." I tasted none
1 Cor. 10.28 — of it, thank God.

That very night, the one
in which their honey I refused, there came
to me while I was sleeping, him whose shame
Mt. 4.1-11 — is everlasting. Satan tested me
severely, and the memory will be
with me so long as in this body I
remain. As if a boulder from the sky
had fallen on me, all my limbs were numb.
But in my ignorance I wonder, from
what quarter came the inspiration to
cry out Helias'[34] name? I wish I knew.
Eph. 5.14 — But in the midst of this I saw the sun
begin to rise in heaven. When I'd begun
again to shout, "Helias!", with all my might,
the sun descended in its brilliant light
and took away the weight from me. Then I
believed that it was Jesus Christ Who my
deliverance had achieved, and that it was
the Spirit of the living God Who caused
me thus to cry, and cried in me. I pray

[34] Patrick is genuinely confused about what led him to cry out, "Helias" (Elijah). However, the Latin, *helios* (sun), may have been what he was seeking, as the context suggests, and Patrick may simply have been exposing his ignorance yet again. Patrick will later refer to Christ as the sun, and this was a frequent theme in later Celtic art, particularly in stone crosses (cf. Jakob Streit, *Sun and Cross* [Edinburgh: Floris Books, 1984], 112).

that it will be so also on the day
Lk. 12.11, 12 of trouble, as the Gospel says, "That day,"
declares the Lord, "the words you need to say
will not arise from you; the Spirit of
the Father, Who provides for you in love,
will speak within you."

[35]So, as I have said
above, we journeyed many days. Instead
of suffering daily depravation, through
them all the Lord provided us with food
and fire and dry conditions. Once, when we
had run out of provisions, mercifully
He brought us to some other people who
supplied our need. And He was gracious to
me all throughout those years before I came
unto my home again. When, on that same
extended journey, I was once again
enslaved and made the prisoner of men,
I spent the first night with my captors. And
I heard a voice that told me, "In the hand
of these your captors you will two months be."[36]
I know it was a word from God to me,
for so it came to pass; the sixteenth night
I was with them, He helped me to take flight
and gain my freedom.

So at last I came[37]

[35] The following paragraph has been rearranged in order to make Patrick's account more strictly chronological.

[36] Perhaps Patrick meant "during two months," that is, part of one month and the next. See on.

[37] Patrick is probably twenty-five or-six years old by the time of his arrival home (lines 473–76).

unto my home in Britain, to that same
familiar country from which I had been
abducted to become a slave of men.
My family rejoiced at my return,
and when my tribulations they had learned,
they begged me, as a son, to stay with them
and never leave our happy home again.
And so, no doubt, I would have been content
to do, but God was pleased I should be spent
in other ways; for while I tarried there
amid my leisure, He worked to prepare
me for a larger task. There came to me
one night a vision. From across the sea
Acts 16.1-10 a man appeared; Victoricus[38] was his name.
He had in his possession as he came
so many letters, and he gave me one
of them. The heading on it left me numb:
"The Voice of the Irish," it proclaimed. As I
began to read the letter, deep in my
imagination in that moment I
could hear the voices of the people by
the wood of Foclut,[39] which is near the sea
in western Ireland, and it seemed to me
that they were crying out, as with one voice,
"O holy servant boy, we would rejoice
for you to come and walk among us." I
was pierced by great emotion, and my eye
could not continue, so I woke. I praise
the Lord that finally, after many days

[38] The specific detail of this name suggests this may have been someone he knew during his time of enslavement.

[39] This is probably the area in which Patrick served as a slave for six years.

and years, he answered their request.[40] Again,
he spoke to me another night, and when
I heard His words—if they were in me or
beside me, only He can know—before
He finished, I was struck with terror, and
His words I simply could not understand,
except for at the end, when He declared,
"The One Who speaks to you is He Who spared
not life on your behalf." And so again,
I saw Him praying hard in me, and then,
as if I were in my own body, I
was hearing Him above me, over my
most inner being, and with groanings hard.
I felt that it could only be the Lord
who interceded thus for me. And all
the while I was dumfounded at His call,
astonished, wondering Who it was Who prayed
so earnestly for me. And then He made
me know He was the Spirit of the Lord.
So I awoke, and I recalled the word
Rom. 8.26 of the Apostle, where He said, "We do
not know how we should make our prayers unto
the Lord; so in our weakness He provides
His Spirit, Who instructs us, and Who guides
and pleads for us in groanings without words."
1 Jn. 2.1 He also says, "Our Advocate, the Lord
on our behalf will intercede." I knew
that moment what He wanted me to do.

[40] Here he is reflecting on his long ministry among the Irish, not on how long it took him to respond to the vision.

# 3. Kept Within His Grace

*To shield me on this day I call: Strong power*
*of seraphim, with angels every hour*
*obeying, and archangels standing by*
*assisting in the glorious company*
*of holy, risen ones, and in the prayers*
*of fathers, and in visions in the air*
*and apostolic words, in annals of*
*the witness of the holy Savior's love,*
*and in the innocence of virgins and*
*the steadfast deeds of every righteous man.*

*To shield me on this day I call: Heaven's might,*
*the brilliance of the sunshine and the white*
*of moon, fire's glory, lightning's swiftness, wind's*
*unbounded wildness, every fathom in*
*the ocean, earth's solidity, and all*
*the steadfast rocks of earth, both great and small.*

I spent some years among the Irish[41] to
prepare[42] myself to follow what I knew

---

[41] I am assuming that Patrick went to Ireland shortly after the vision recorded in lines 597–511. See note 6, Prologue, and note 14, Section I.

[42] Calvin provides a useful summary of the process whereby a man became a priest during the period of the early Church. Something like this probably was still observed in Patrick's time (*Institutes of the Christian Religion*, IV.iv.9): "from early youth under sacred instruction and strict training they took on an

to be my calling from the Lord. It was
not I who made this choice to go, because,
as I have said, the Lord was calling me.
And at the time I came across the sea
I barely knew the Lord, though He was dear
to me. And this was good, for it was clear
He would reform and shape me and prepare
me so that I might serve His sheep and care
for all His flocks, as I am doing yet
today. And so, though once I would not let
my mind consider all my own need of
His saving mercy, now the Father's love
for others is my care and my concern.

There was so much that I would need to learn,

exemplary life of gravity and holiness; and, separated from worldly cares, they became accustomed to spiritual cares and studies. But, just as army recruits are instructed through sham battles for real and earnest conflict, so were there definite rudiments in which they were trained as clerics before they were promoted to the offices proper. First, then, they were entrusted with opening and closing of the church, and were called 'doorkeepers.' Afterward they were called 'acolytes,' to assist the bishop in household tasks and continually to accompany him, first for honor's sake, then that no suspicion might arise. Moreover, that they might gradually become known to the people and acquire commendation for themselves, and at the same time learn to be seen by all and to speak before all; that, when made presbyters, they might not be covered with shame when they came forward to teach – they were given opportunity to read from the pulpit. In this way, to prove their diligence in individual exercises, they were promoted by degrees until they were made sub-deacons" (John T. McNeill, ed., Ford Lewis Battles, tr., *The Library of Christian Classics* [Philadelphia: The Westminster Press, 1960). It is interesting to note in Patrick's case that his lack of "formal education" did not disqualify from him from being accepted into training for the office of minister of the Gospel.

and much that I would never understand.[43]
I studied and I served the Savior, and
in time I was ordained a priest.[44] But when
my name as bishop was suggested, then
I was attacked by certain ones among
my seniors. It was not that I was young
that they opposed me, but they made their case
against me—mind you, not before my face,
but in my absence[45]—for a youthful sin.
And on that shameful day did I begin
to be so strongly tempted that I might
have fallen, yes, both here and in the night
of all eternity; but God showed me
His mercy, me this humble exile. He
2 Cor. 12.9 came mightily to bolster me and to
support me till this dreadful trial was through.
For it was not through me that this disgrace
and scandal came to light before the face
of God and men. And yet I pray God will
not hold this act of sin against them still.[46]
They found a pretext from some thirty years
before, and brought against me to my tears
and sorrow a confession I had told
unto my friend before I came to hold
the deacon's office, which I told to him

[43] See his previous comments about his paltry education in Section I, lines 187–204.

[44] But not before having been first a deacon, line 599.

[45] Patrick was apparently serving as a priest in Ireland when his name was put forward to fill the vacancy in the office of bishop by his superiors in Britain. On this first occasion, however, he was rejected, as he will explain.

[46] He is clearly of the opinion that his superiors sinned in allowing this childhood sin to be their reason for rejecting him, although he does not hold it against them.

when I was in a melancholy, grim,
and anxious state of mind. When I was just
a boy, before I knew the Lord—I must
have been fifteen—one day, indeed, one hour
I yielded to temptation's awful power,
and it was this, as I believe, that found
me taken from my home to Ireland, bound
Heb. 12.6 in chains. The Lord chastised me for my sin,
and now it was before me yet again,
impeding my appointment. So I was
rejected by my seniors, and because
of this was my episcopate delayed.
But God Who called me to this labor stayed
beside me, so that on that very night
He came to me within a dream; and right
before me were the documents that caused
my shame and my dishonor. But He paused
not, saying, "It displeases Us to see
Our chosen one thus stripped of honor." He
said not, "displeases Me," but "Us," as though
He linked Himself with me, that I might know
that I was still His choice, as if He said,
Zech. 2.8 "Whoever touches you, or harms your head,
has touched the apple of My eye." And so
I offer thanks to Him Who made me know
His mercy and Who strengthened me in all
my weaknesses, for He did not recall
me from my place of exile for His Name,[47]
but showed His favor in the works I came
to do, and which I from the Lord had learned.
And so, much more I felt His power had turned
my shame to vindication in the face

---

[47] Although, as he testified, his disappointment was such that he almost fell away, God sustained him, and he stayed on in Ireland as a priest.

of God and men.[48] Though I cannot erase
what I have done, I tell you boldly that
my conscience does no more reproach me at
this matter. As the Lord is witness, I
do not deceive in what I say, nor lie.

But I am sorry for my friend: For how
did we deserve that he should bring just now
this evidence against me? He to whom
I had my soul entrusted! He had room
within his heart for me before this case
was mooted (for I was not in that place
when my transgression was discussed); for he
had worked that they should offer me the see[49]
of Ireland, and had told me once, "You should
be made a bishop," though I was not good
or worthy of this calling. How did he,
a short time later, turn his back on me,
before men good and bad, to bring me to
disgrace for what I shared with him, he who
forgave me willingly and gladly, just
as God Himself had done, in Whom I trust,
Rom. 8.33, 34 and Who is greater than the rest?

I will
belabor my disgrace no longer. Still,
Mt. 5.15 I must not hide the gift of God, which He
so graciously and freely gave to me
when I was captive here in Ireland. For
it was when I was yet a slave, for more
than six long years, that I with tears then sought

[48] That is, because he stayed on, prospered in his ministry, and was ultimately appointed to the episcopacy on a subsequent occasion.

[49] That is, the episcopacy.

Him strenuously, and found Him—as I ought
to have done much sooner on. He saved me from
my sins, and now His Holy Spirit has come
to dwell within me, as I now believe;
and He is pleased my labors to receive
unto this day. And though I may sound bold
in this, I am convinced the voice that told
me to continue here was from the Lord,
and not from men. For if it were the word
of men alone that brought me here, I could
not speak for Him, as every Christian should.

And so I thank my God untiringly,
Who on the day that I was tried kept me
within His grace, so that today I may
present unto my Lord in every way
the sacrifice of my own soul. For He
has saved me through my trials, thus causing me
to ask, "Who am I, Lord, what must I do,
that in Your majesty and mercy You
have shown Yourself to me, so that today
I magnify Your holy Name and say
among the heathen, all throughout this land,
that You alone are Lord, and in Your hand
are all our times, both good and bad?" And so
whatever comes, though good or bad, I go
in gratitude and faith to serve the Lord,
Who taught me how to find within His Word
Rom. 10.17 the faith I need to follow Him, and Who
has helped me, ignorant as I am, to do
this holy work to which at last I came,[50]
to bring the Irish to obey to His Name.
It is as if I were a follower of

[50] The office of bishop of Ireland.

those glorious ones of whom the God of love
foretold in former times, that they would be
the harbingers of Gospel grace that He
would send as witnesses before all men
Mt. 24.14 before this dying world should reach its end.[51]
And we have seen this done, for we have preached
Rom. 15.20 where never had before the Gospel reached,
and we have offered what He freely gives
to places that, beyond which, no one lives.[52]
So this alone I boast, and nothing more:
That I, a rustic man, who was before
a wretched sinner and a slave, have been
exalted to proclaim God's Word to men.

---

[51] Once again we can see that Patrick's burden was fueled in no small part by millenarian expectations.

[52] Ireland was considered the ends of the earth, so far as anyone knew. Patrick emphasizes the evangelistic nature of his episcopacy, that he did not merely seek to shepherd those who already knew the Lord, nor content himself with administrative minutiae, but pressed on throughout much of Ireland to preach the Gospel to those who had never heard it. As Thompson points out, this was an altogether different approach to episcopal ministry than was typically practiced among the churches of the Roman world, and may have been the unspoken cause of much of the criticism he received at times in his ministry (Thompson, 80, 81).

# 4. Undertaking for the Lord

*This day I call to me God's strength to show*
*my way, God's power to help me as I go;*
*God's wisdom for my guide, His holy eye*
*to light my way, His ear to hear my cry;*
*God's Word to fill my speaking, and His hand*
*to hold me as I go, and help me stand;*
*His path before me and His shield to guard*
*me; all His strong angelic legions hard*
*around me to protect me: from the snares*
*of demons, from temptation's might, from cares*
*and worries, and from threats of nature, from*
*one man or many that may seek to come*
*for my destruction, whether from afar*
*or near, no matter who or where they are.*

I know it would be tedious to tell
in whole or in detail, as very well
I might, my undertaking for the Lord.
But here I shall relate in brief a word
concerning how the holy God, on more
than one occasion, intervening for
my benefit, freed me from slavery
and from the dangers that have threatened me
throughout my ministry, as well as from
the many snares and troubles that have come

my way.[53] I do not wish my readers to
Ps. 139.16 affront, but God, Who knows what we will do
and everything that comes to pass before
it does, is my authority, and more
than once He gave me counsel,[54] just because
I'm in His care, although He knew I was
both poor and insignificant.

From where
did all this understanding come to bear
on me, who neither knew the number of
my days on earth nor Him Who showed His love
to me?[55] How did I come to know the Lord,
Eph. 2.8, 9 if not through grace alone, and by His Word,
that I should long to follow Him and leave
my homeland and my family to grieve
for me? When first I left for Ireland's shore
they offered many gifts and tears and more
to keep me home; and I offended them
and went against the wishes of the men
who were accountable for me.[56] But I
was guided by the Lord above in my
decision, and He told me I should not
Gal. 2.3-5 agree with them or give consent to what
they wanted. He opposed them all on my
behalf and triumphed in my soul, so I

[53] Curiously, Patrick never fulfills this promise.

[54] Patrick continues to assert that God led him in all that he did.

[55] That is, when he was still a rebellious youth.

[56] Patrick went to Ireland on his own, without the permission or support of ecclesiastical authorities, and even against their judgment. See on, lines 950–957. Apparently they did not forbid his going to Ireland – since they had no ecclesiastical jurisdiction over him, other than as a church member – but they counseled against it.

can take no credit for my leaving. So
I came to Ireland so that I might go
among the heathen and proclaim the Word
of God and call them to receive the Lord,
and suffer many insults at their hands.
So it is difficult to understand
the sad disgrace of my rejection, when
I suffered so much at the hands of men,
including being made a slave again
Phil. 3.7, 8 and sacrificing my inheritance[57]
to serve the pagans.[58] I am ready though
Acts 21.13 to freely give my life that they might know
my Savior, so in Ireland I will stay
and serve the Lord, until my dying day!

Because I owe so much to God. He gave
me this great boon: That through me He would save
so many heathen, who would be confirmed
as followers of Christ; that in my term
a clergy should be raised to care for them—
so many thousands of the finest men[59]
of Ireland; and that churches by the scores
of hundreds should be built, where men adore
the Lord of glory; and that thousands should

---

[57] Patrick's father was a decurion, the Roman equivalent of a tax-collector. This was a hereditary office, from which Patrick was excused because of his decision to go into the ministry. He also seems to have liquidated whatever inheritance he was to receive in order to fund his ministry.

[58] In this sentence Patrick appears to be referring to his initial rejection for the office of bishop, after he had managed to attain to the priesthood and had established a proven ministry among the Irish.

[59] Lines 770–773 draw on the *Annals of the Four Masters* (17th century) and *The Book of Armagh* (7th century) (De Paor, 129, 198).

be taught to read the Scriptures,[60] that the good
and perfect will of God they might discern,
that they to follow Him in love might learn.
The Lord redeemed this holy people from
the ends of earth, just as He said through some
Jer. 16.19 of the prophetic writings, "All your vain
and empty idols are to you no gain
Acts 13.47 at all." Again, "For I have placed you for
a light among the nations ever more,
that you might bring salvation to the ends
of all the earth." And all of this depends
on Him, and on His mercy, not on me.

And so, rejected, I resolved to be
about my ministry and wait upon
the Lord to make His promises to dawn
on me. For He will never fail in these,
Lk. 13.29 as it is stated in the Gospel, "East
and west shall come and will recline here at
the table" where the patriarch Abram sat
with Isaac and with Jacob. We believe
from every nation men will come and grieve
for their iniquities and will receive
the Lord. And furthermore do we believe
it is our obligation from the Lord
to diligently fish for men. His Word
Mt. 4.19 is clear: "Come follow Me and I will make
you fish for men." In this you'll see I take
Jer. 16.16 Him at His Word: "Behold, I'm sending out
so many fishermen and hunters." Doubt
it not; it is His Word. From which you see
it is most clear, that all who wish to be
His followers are obliged to cast their nets

[60] As part of his ministry Patrick taught letters and reading to those he disciplined.

to catch a multitude of fish and get
a mighty gathering for the Lord. So there
should be sufficient clergy everywhere
to baptize and to preach, because the need
is great among the people. We must heed
Mt. 28.19, 20 the Savior's Word, Who teaches us to "Go
and make disciples of all nations, so
that they might be baptized into the Name
of Father, Son, and Spirit. Teach the same
to follow all that I have taught, and see,
until the world is ended I will be
Mk. 16.15, 16 with you." Again He says, "Go into all
the world, and preach to every creature, small
and great; and all who will believe and be
baptized shall know My saving mercy: he,
however, who does not believe, will be
condemned." And in another passage He
Mt. 24.14 declares, "This Gospel of the Kingdom will
be preached to all throughout the world until
it testifies to every man, and then
the end will come." And through the prophet's pen
Joel 2.28 the Lord foretells, "And it shall come to pass,
I will pour out My Spirit in the last
days over all mankind. Your daughters and
your sons will prophesy, and I will send
your young men visions and your old men dreams;
and in those days, when all around it seems
that darkness is descending, I will pour
My Holy Spirit out upon all your
own servants, male and female, and they all
will prophesy." Hosea, you recall,
Hos. 1.10 declared, "A people not My own shall be
My people called, and will obtain from Me
the mercy of the Lord. And it shall be
that in that place where it is said, 'To Me

you are no people,' there shall they be called
'the children of the living God.'" So all
that we have seen in Ireland in these days
has come to pass because of what it says
in Holy Scripture. God is faithful to
His Word, and so this heathen people who
no knowledge of the Savior had before,
but worshipped idols, demons, cults, and more,
have come to be the people of the Lord,
Who rescued them according to His Word
of promise. Irish sons and daughters, yes,
and even royal children—thousands bless
the name of Jesus. Many have become
obedient to the Lord, receiving from
Him mercy to become the virgins and
the monks of Jesus Christ. So understand,
it is His faithfulness these many years,
enabling us to overcome our fears
and troubles, that has brought this harvest to
the Lord of glory.

Let one instance do
for now: There was an Irish woman who
was of nobility, both lovely to
behold, and most mature, whom I baptized.
She came to us thereafter and apprised
us that she had received a message from
an angel of the Lord,[61] and he had come

[61] As with his own dreams and visions, while they may be extraordinary, Patrick does not consider them unheard of as means of discerning God's leading. Indeed, in this story, which bears similarities to his own situation, the vision (or dream) was decisive for the woman who took a vow of virginity, knowing the suffering this would entail.

to call her to become a virgin[62] of
the Lord, and know and serve Him in His love
according to this ministry. Thanks be
to God, just six days after this and she,
in a most excellent and eager way,
embraced this way of life which all obey
who are the virgins of the Lord. This life
they undertake with suffering and with strife,
especially from their parents who do not
believe. For accusations false are brought
against them, and harassment sore, because
they give themselves unto the virgins' laws
against their fathers' will. But nonetheless
their numbers grow, and God is pleased to bless
the British women here among us, too,
as well as many of the widows who
take vows of chastity. But those who slaves
among the pagans are, and whom God saves,
endure the most, for constant fears beset
them, and they suffer from continual threats
from fellow slaves and masters. But the Lord
has given grace that they might walk before
Him bravely, imitating Him in spite
of many prohibitions.

In the light
of this, I could not go to Britain now
Neh. 6.1-3 to make my own defense,[63] explaining how

[62] Probably not to become a nun; rather, this seems to have been a perpetual vow of virginity in order to devote oneself to the service of the Lord in various ways.

[63] He may either have been summoned by his superiors or urged by his colleagues to go to Britain in order either to answer the charges against him or to put them to rest once and for all. He was not willing to do this for the reasons he states, and offers his *Confession* rather like a deposition in his defense.

the Lord has used my work and answering those
who criticize me, even if I chose
to go, or if I wished to leave these sheep
(although, within my heart of hearts, I weep
to see my homeland and my kin, and would
go even unto Gaul to see the good
work God has done there and the brethren greet—
the Lord knows such a journey would be sweet
to me). But I am by the Spirit bound,
that if I leave this work, I will be found
a guilty servant on that day. And so
I fear this work would suffer should I go
to Britain now. And not just I, but He
Who has commanded me to come and be
among these people for the rest of all
my days: I pray that He Who gave this call
to me will guard me from all evil, so
that I may not against His counsel know
transgression.

So I hope that I have done
just what I should have, and that everyone
might know that in myself I put no trust
as long as I am in this body. Just
as surely do I know that he who strives
each day to turn me from the faith that thrives
in me, and from the teachings of the true
religion, which I zealously hold to
until my dying day for Jesus' sake,
1 Pt. 5.8 is powerful. The enemy would make
me satisfy my flesh, and drag me off
to death, enticing me to sin and scoff
the Law of God.[64] I know that, unlike some

[64] Patrick appears to believe that Satan is tempting him to leave the field and go to Britain for the sole purpose of defending his good name.

believers, I imperfect am.[65] Far from
me, brethren, to deny it. But the Lord
forgives me, and I have no shame toward
my Savior. Since I learned to know Him in
my youth, the love and fear of God within
me have increased, and I have to this day,
His help attending me along the way,
been faithful to Him. Let them scoff and laugh
who will. But I must on the Lord's behalf
speak out to show the signs and wonders He
throughout these many years has shown to me
before they happened. For our Savior knows
Amos 3.7, 8 before all things what comes to pass, and shows
them to His servants.[66]

That is why I give
unceasing thanks to Him while I still live,
for He has often lenient been with all
my foolishness and carelessness. I call
on Him to judge. For He with me has not
been wrathful, who was given to and taught
by Him to be His helper, but was slow
to take this holy task in hand and go
as He commanded and the Spirit led.[67]
The Lord took pity on me, as I said,
because He knew I was not ready for
this high and holy calling.[68] And so more

[65] This seems like a not-so-subtle swipe at his critics.

[66] While we do not see any prophesy in Patrick's ministry – that is, until the later *Lives* – he obviously believed it was still a valid gift, and seemed to think his superiors and colleagues would not chafe at such an idea.

[67] It is not clear what Patrick intends here, unless he tarried longer in Britain before coming to Ireland than he now feels he should have.

[68] At this point in the *Confession* Patrick admits that he lacked administrative skills such as a bishop would require when he was first considered for the office.

than once He bore with me. And many sought
to hinder this endeavor, saying, "Ought
a fellow such as this to danger go
among the enemies who do not know
the Lord?" Yet not from malice spoke they thus;
they did not like the look of it. I trust
you'll understand my point: I think that they
were hesitating at my naiveté.
And I was not unmindful of the grace
at work in me, and should have given place
to them more readily.[69]

So this is then
my simple explanation to those men
and brethren—fellow servants—who in me
Gal. 2.2 believed because of what they[70] saw to be
in me by what I preached—and still today
continue to proclaim—so that you may
be strengthened and confirmed in your belief.
And O, what satisfaction, what relief,
you would afford me if you too could be
persuaded to do better![71] As for me,
Prov. 1.10 let this be my renown: "The wisdom of
the son gives honor to the father's love."

---

[69] Perhaps he means that he should have listened to their advice and stayed in Britain to take his training. This seems to be a gesture of conciliation, and nothing more, since elsewhere he does not second-guess the Lord's leading in coming to Ireland when he did.

[70] His colleagues in Ireland, who observed his ministry at firsthand, confirmed him to the priesthood, and were now under his care as their bishop.

[71] Patrick suggests that, rather than waste their time listening to what they know to be scurrilous and ungrounded accusations, his colleagues should follow his example and devote themselves more earnestly to the work of ministry.

# 5. A Man of Full Integrity[72]

*Around me now I gather all these powers*
*to save my soul and body in their hours*
*of need from all the forces that assail*
*me: Prophets false and pagan myth and tale,*
*heretical deceit, false gods around*
*me everywhere. Against all spells cast down*
*by women, blacksmiths, Druids; unlawful things*
*that hurt the body, and the spirit sting.*

1 Cor. 2.1-5

You know, and so does God, how I have been
among you since my youth[73] in truth and in
sincerity of faith and heart. And I
have kept my faith, and will until I die,
although I live among the heathen. And
the Lord knows I have not deceived a man
of them, nor even thought of doing so,
lest I should persecution cause to grow
against the Savior and His Church, and all

[72] In this, the shortest section of his *Confession*, Patrick tackles head-on the charge against him, that he was laboring at his ministry in Ireland principally for financial gain. His response is direct and concise, and he calls on his readers to consider their own experience of him in their midst.

[73] This reference to his youth would seem to support the idea that Patrick came to Ireland while he was still a young man.

of us,[74] and lest the Name of God should fall
to blasphemy because of me. The Word
Lev. 24.16 — of God declares, "The man who to the Lord
brings blasphemy is cursed." And it is true,
though I lack any skill, I've tried to do
1 Thess. 5.22 — all that I could to guard myself in all
my dealings, so that none could ever call
me greedy. Even with the brethren and
the virgins of the Lord I took a stand
that I would not receive the gifts that they
would give to me. At times they'd even lay
them on the altar; I returned them all,
no matter if the gifts were great or small.
And so, not understanding why I did
this, they became offended. But I bid
Mt. 6.19, 20 — you understand, I hoped eternity
to gain, and so I labored hard to be
1 Tim. 3.7; — a man of full integrity in all
1 Pt. 2.15; 4.15 — my dealings, being careful not to fall
into temptation, lest the pagans should
some pretext have to denigrate my good
episcopate and to disparage me.

Perhaps you're thinking that it just may be
I baptized all those thousands so that I
might fill my bulging purse and prosper by
this ministry? Well, not so much as half
a penny crossed my palms, just ask my staff.
Or when the Lord through ordinary me
ordained those many thousand men to be
His priests and deacons, which I did for free—

[74] He may be referring here to other Britons in Ireland – slaves and other expatriates – who, while they were not yet believers, would nonetheless have been implicated with him in any scandal he might have caused.

if any one of them accuses me
of taking even what it costs to buy
a single shoe, then let him speak, and I
will give it back to him.

In fact, I spent
on your behalf, no matter where I went
throughout my ministry, that I might be
received.[75] I crossed this land from sea to sea,
to every tribe and all the outermost
domains, where nothing is, that I might boast
about the Lord, to places none had gone
Rom. 15.20 before to baptize or ordain, where none
among the people was confirmed. So by
the grace of God alone I say that I
achieved all these results, both gladly and
with full integrity, that you might stand
today within His saving grace.

You know,
I gave gifts to the local chieftains, so
that I might minister among them. And
these fees did not include, you understand,
the stipends that I freely gave their sons
Acts 20.34 to travel with me.[76] These were my own funds

[75] Apparently, Patrick paid fees to the local kings as he came into their domains in order that he might go freely among the people to preach to them. These were not bribes in the strictest sense, since Patrick had no self-interest in mind.

[76] As people came to Christ, Patrick, following the example of Paul, would select certain ones of them to travel with him, so that he might further disciple them and prepare them for ministry as officers in the churches he started. These men had to be supported, and Patrick undertook the responsibility of providing their support himself.

which were for their support employed. And still,
on one occasion they[77] designed to kill
me, when they seized me from among my friends.
But God had not ordained for me an end
of life just yet. And though they stole from us
all that we had, and chained me, still our trust
in God remained; and on the fourteenth day
2 Pt. 2.9 of my captivity, He made a way
for my release and the return of all
our goods. Firm friends, who had the call
of Jesus followed, intervened on our
behalf, and drawing on the Savior's power
effected our deliverance.[78] Furthermore,
you know yourselves, since you have seen before,
how much I paid to local magistrates
in all the districts where I served the great
and small alike. The total I have spent
to be allowed to preach wherever I went
is very great indeed: I'd say no less
than what a man would have to pay to bless
some fifteen slaves with freedom.[79] This was done
so that the Kingdom work we had begun
among you might continue. I have no
regret in this, and still am doing so
unto this day. I still will spend that I

[77] That is, certain local rulers.

[78] It is not unlikely that these friends redeemed Patrick from slavery through a financial payment, a common practice in those days.

[79] Thompson points out (99) that this would have been an enormous sum, even if it represents the total of what Patrick expended throughout the course of his ministry in order to gain access for preaching and support those whom he was preparing for ministry. The total comes to something around 150 years' wages for a common man.

may do this work until the day I die.
That men may know the Savior Who controls
2 Cor. 12.15 the world, I'll spend myself to save their souls.

# 6. Bishop to the Irish People

*Be Christ my strong Protector on this day*
*against the threat of poison on the way,*
*or burning, drowning, wounding: Through reward*
*and plenty, Christ beside me, Christ the Lord*
*before me, Christ behind me, Christ within*
*me; Christ beneath me, Christ above me; Him*
*at my right hand, and on the left of me;*
*Christ in my lying, sitting, rising be;*
*Christ in the heart of all who know and care*
*for me, upon the tongue of all who share*
*a word with me; Christ in the eye of all*
*who see me, in their ear to whom I call.*

One further incident will I relate:[80]
Though I am but a sinner and not great
in learning, yet I am a bishop to
the Irish people, charged to care and do
for them all that I can that they might know
the saving mercy of the Lord. And so
I readily admit, that what I am

---

[80] This section contains Patrick's *Letter Against the Soldiers of Coroticus*, which he sent as a letter of excommunication against a British ruler and his soldiers who had acted violently against some new Christians. All the arguments that Patrick musters here are to support his case in issuing this declaration of excommunication and calling on the people to whom he ministered to stand by it.

is of the Lord. According to His plan
for me I live among barbarians,
and so I know the ways of all these sons
of demons. And when one of them, who claimed
to be a Christian—Coroticus[81] was his name—
attacked the flock of God, I wrote to him
a letter, stern and harsh, and very grim,
which I include below. And I would not
have chosen to address him so, but ought
to have, because the zeal of God compelled
me, and the saving truth of Christ impelled,
me, as did love for those who suffered. Some
may look askance to read this letter from
my hand, but I regard it not. I live
to teach the heathen, though they may not give
attention to me. And this letter stands
as testimony from this bishop's hand
that, having left my home and family
to serve among them, I would gladly be
deprived of life itself, if duty led:
Here then the letter, and the words I said:

"With my own hand have I these words set out
and written—let the readers have no doubt
that they are from the hand of Patrick—to
be sent, transmitted and delivered through
the bearer to the soldiers of the chief
Coroticus—a murderer and a thief—
Eph. 2.12 no fellow citizens of mine or of

[81] Thompson (125 ff.) strikes me as having the best understanding of Coroticus and Patrick's *Letter*. Coroticus was apparently a British ruler living in Ireland, whom Patrick knew and who claimed to be a Christian, along with all his subjects.

the holy Romans;[82] they are men in love
with demons, as their evil deeds make clear.
They live in death, like Satan, and hold dear
1 Jn. 2.15 the friendship of apostate Picts and Scots.
I now denounce them, men who would besot
themselves with Christian blood, who took the lives
of innocent believers whom I strive
to bring to life in countless numbers for
the Lord and to confirm in Him.

"Before
the catachumens could remove their white
baptismal robes, and while the oil[83] shone bright
upon their brows, then they were slaughtered and
cut down by those whom I have mentioned. Man
and woman, young and old, they felt the sword.
I sent a priest and clerics with a word
requesting they return some of the loot
and all the captives to us. With loud hoots
of laughter they rejected our request.

"Because of this I know not if it's best
to weep for those who have been killed or who
were carried off, or those who have fallen to
the clutches of the Evil One.[84] For they
Rev. 20.14, 15 will burn with him in hell on judgment day,
Rom. 6.16 since he who sins becomes a slave, a son
of Satan.

---

[82] Patrick intimates that, by their vicious deeds, Coroticus and his soldiers have shown that they are not, in fact, Christians, as they claimed.

[83] Apparently the violence occurred shortly after this group of believers had been baptized. They had not even been able to get out of their baptismal robes, and the oil applied to their foreheads as part of baptism was still glistening.

[84] That is, Coroticus and his soldiers.

"Therefore now, let everyone
who fears the Lord be sure to understand,
that they—who killed our kin and raised their hand
against their brethren, ravening wolves who fed
upon God's people like a meal of bread—
are strangers to me, and to God. For I
am His ambassador. As it is by
Ps. 119.53 the psalmist said, 'The wicked have Your Word
destroyed, O Lord', that holy law the Lord
has planted graciously and with success
among us at the end of time, to bless
and keep us here in Ireland. By His grace
it has been firmly founded in this place.

"My jurisdiction I do not exceed.[85]
For I am one of those God has decreed
to preach the Gospel even to the end
of the earth, though persecution from that friend
of Satan, who fears neither God nor us,
God's holy priests, I mean Coroticus,
should come my way. God chose me and He gave
Mt. 16.19 me full authority the lost to save
and to debar the wicked from the gate
of heaven.

[86]"And so I say to all, the great
and small alike, all you who holy are

---

[85] This is one of the statements that leads Thompson to believe, contrary to others, that Coroticus was living in Ireland and not Scotland. Patrick claims to have been acting within the bounds of his ecclesiastical jurisdiction as Bishop of Ireland. He could not have exercised the discipline of excommunication against someone outside his own parish.

[86] Here through line 1175 we see something of what excommunication meant.

and pure of heart, though you be near or far
away, I now forbid you to bestow
upon these cowards any help, or show
1 Cor. 5.9-11 them any honor. Do not eat or drink
with them; accept from them no alms. And think
no more of them as brethren till they show
repentance for their crimes and let them go
whom they in vile captivity detain.
For God rejects the gifts of wicked, vain,
deceitful men, who offer from the poor
2 Sam. 12.1-7 man's goods their sacrifice to God. Be sure,
they're like the man who in the father's sight
would sacrifice his son.

"That word is right
Job 20.15-27 which says, 'His wealth unjustly gained will be
regurgitated from his belly; he
shall by the angel of death be dragged away;
the rage of dragons will consume his day;
the adder's tongue will kill him; on a pyre
he'll perish, in an all-consuming fire.'
Hab. 2.6 Again, 'Woe unto them who fill themselves
Mt. 16.26 with that which is not theirs,' and 'He who delves
into the world for profit, though he gain
the whole, shall lose his soul and know the pain
of loss.' Yet tedious would it be to show
from all the Law what any man can know
who reads it: Avarice is a mortal sin.
Ex. 20.17 'You shall in no way covet what is in
Ex. 20.13 your neighbor's hand.' 'You shall not kill.' For he
who murders cannot with the Savior be.
1 Jn. 3.15 'Who hates his brother kills,' or, we may say,
1 Jn. 3.10 'Who does not love his brother walks the way
of death.'

"So how much greater is the crime
of him who kills his brother in the prime
of life, when he has only recently
been won to Christ, has just begun to be
a follower of the Lord because he heard
the most unworthy preaching of the Word
from my own lips? Was it apart from God's
direction that I came to Ireland, trod
this land, and have converted many? Who
was it that drove me? I am sure that you
will see the Spirit has prevented me
from seeing any of my family
again, that I might here remain. From me
comes forth this mercy that has let me be
a servant to the very people who
enslaved me once, who showed such malice to
my father's servants? Not from me, but from
the Lord of mercy; it's by Him I've come
to Ireland, who a gentleman had been,
that is, considered by the eyes of men,
the son of a decurion.[87] And I
have sold all my patrimony, and why?
That I might be of service here. And yet
I have no shame in this, and no regret.
I serve the Savior on behalf of this,
a people foreign to me, that the bliss
of His salvation they might know, that He
might ever more enshrined in glory be.
And if those people who are of my race[88]
treat me contemptuously, and with disgrace,
then is that Word fulfilled which testifies,

[87] That is, a collector of revenue.

[88] Coroticus: Another statement upon which Thomspon builds his case for Coroticus being a Briton ruling in part of northeast Ireland.

Mt. 13.57 'The honor of a prophet surely lies
beyond his native land.'

"Thus it appears
we are of different folds; for it is clear
these sons of demons worship not the Lord
Who testifies against them in His Word,
Mt. 12.30 which also says, 'He is against me who
is not with me; and he who will not do
the work of gathering has become to Me
a scatterer of my harvest.' So you see,
it makes no sense: While one destroys, one builds.
One sought to save the lost; the other killed
the holy ones of God. I do not ask
for what is mine. I am about the task
which God has given me, Who in His love
and kindness, called on me to be one of
his fishermen and hunters, whom He said
He would raise up to bring new life to dead
men in these latter days.

"And yet it seems
my ministry receives not the esteem
it should, for I am treated with contempt.[89]
My sheep are mangled, stolen by unkempt,
uncouth, ungodly robbers in the hire
of this Coroticus, who put this fire
within them and who orders them about.[90]

---

[89] A subtle admonition to the readers of this letter not to make the same mistake that Coroticus did, who is herewith being excommunicated along with his soldiers, by showing contempt for Patrick's ministry. By this admonition Patrick intends to strengthen support for his action on the part of his readers.

[90] It appears that Coroticus may not have been present himself at the slaughter; however, he did command it.

Far from the love of God, this wicked lout
betrays God's children to the hands of Picts
and pagan Irish. Savage wolves, and sick
with sin, they thus devour God's flock, just when,
by sovereign care, that flock of newborn men
had reached its greatest growth within this land.
I cannot count the sons of the Irish and
the royal daughters who have now become
for Christ both monks and virgins. Therefore, from
this evidence I urge you, do not see
this injury which has been done to me
and to my ministry as just. For it
is unacceptable, unto the pit
of hell.

"Thus, who among the holy would
not horrified be to offer any good
or think of making merry with the likes
of them? They fill their days with vicious strikes
against the people of the Lord. They live
by plundering the dead, and do not give
a second thought to what they do. And to
their friends and children they give poisonous food,
and do not understand the wickedness
Gn. 3.1-6 in what they do. Like Eve, they think to bless
themselves; instead, they offer death to those
they love. And so it is with him who knows
Jms. 4.17 to do what's right, but chooses evil. He
condemns himself unto eternity.

"This is the custom Christian Roman Gaul
pursues: They send unto the Franks and all
the other heathen worthy holy men
to purchase from captivity again

their baptized captives.[91] On the other hand,
Coroticus and all his wicked band
destroy and sell them to a foreign land,
to people who know not the Savior and
His gracious ways. He might as well have sold
them to a brothel. Yet, you are so bold
to think that you have hope in God! What kind
of hope should anyone expect to find
who does such things, or, for that matter, who
consents and goes along or speaks to you
respectfully? For as the Scripture says,
Rom. 1.32 'Not only those who follow evil ways,
but even those consenting with them shall
be damned.'[92]

"I do not know what more to tell
of those dead children who were direly by
Rom. 12.15 the sword struck down. The Scriptures tell us, 'Cry
1 Cor. 12.26 with those who cry,' and, 'If in sorrow one
of you is found, then sorrow all.' For sons
and daughters who were carried off as slaves
to pagan lands, where open, shameless, grave
iniquity abounds, the Church thus mourns
and offers its lament. Those people scorn
the ways of freedom, those apostate Picts;
and so we mourn our brethren; we are sick
at heart for their captivity, and cry
in grief and sadness, 'Loving brethren I
have led to know the Lord, what can I do

[91] Patrick shows that his first attempt to deal with Coroticus (lines 1135–38) was strictly in accord with accepted practice among continental Christians. This reference leads many to conclude that Patrick was familiar with Gaulish practice because he had been there at some time.

[92] A warning to his readers not to take their stand with the villains.

for you? I am inadequate unto
the task, and have no help to offer man
or God. Perhaps they do not understand
Eph. 4.4-6 that we possess one baptism, and we know
one God. For them it is a matter so
disgraceful that we're Irish.' But you know
the saying, 'Have you not one God? And so,
why have you, one and all, abandoned your
own neighbor?'

"For this reason, grieving for
you, I grieve yet, my loved ones. But again,
within me I rejoice, for not in vain
have I been laboring in your midst. And my
long exile has not been for naught. For I
decry this awful crime that has been done
among us; but remember, every one
of those who died was baptized, and has gone
to paradise. I see you, friends, there on
your journey to the place where neither night
nor death nor dread nor sorrow will affright
you ever; freed from all your bonds, you leap
about like calves, and crush beneath your feet
the wicked, who will be as ashes. You
will reign with the apostles; prophets, too,
and martyrs rule beside you. You will gain
an everlasting kingdom when your pain
is through, as He Himself has promised. He
Lk. 14.28, 29 has said, 'From east and west into the tree
of Abraham shall many come, and they
Rev. 22.15 will sleep within My Kingdom.' 'In the way
without are dogs, the wicked, murderers,'
and elsewhere, 'Every lying perjurer
Rev. 21.8 shall be allotted to the fiery lake.'
Not without reason does the apostle make

1 Pt. 4.18 this statement: 'When the just man barely can
be saved, where does that leave the sinful man,
and him who breaks God's Law?'

"Where then will he—
Coroticus—and all his henchmen see
themselves, these rebels who oppose the rule
of Christ, and show that they are really fools,
and not among His faithful, who have sold
as prizes Christian girls to gain the cold
rewards of worldiness, which all will in
Ps. 83.13, 14 an instant pass? Like mist, or like a thin
smoke trail, which by the wind is soon dispersed,
deceitful sinners will to Christ rehearse
their wretched deeds, and perish in His face.
But for the holy just, another place
has been reserved, for they, in perfect peace
and harmony, eternally shall feast
before the Lord, and sit in judgment on
the nations when this wicked age is done,
and rule over wicked kings forever.

"I
bear witness to the Lord, in spite of my
slight learning, it shall be as I have said.
For do not think these word are mine; instead,
hear what the prophets and apostles say:
Jn. 3.18 'He will be saved who has believed, but they
shall be condemned who do not trust the Lord.'
The Lord has spoken in His holy Word.

"So earnestly I ask each servant of
the Lord, if he is willing, if the love
of God constrains him, bear this letter, so
that no one may pretend he does not know

what I have written; read these words aloud
in public, in the presence of the proud
Coroticus himself. Because if some
time God may in His mercy, let them come
unto their senses and return to Him,
repenting of their gruesome, cruel, and grim
iniquity—however late—if they
should come to hate and loathe their murderous way
of life, and set their prisoners free, then may
they know His mercy, and again obey
His Word, and by repentance show that they
have been restored unto Christ's holy way.

"Now, in the Father, Son, and Spirit, peace
be unto you, and may His grace increase."

# 7. His Ambassador

*I call this day to shield and shelter me*
*a mighty power, the Holy Trinity!*
*His threeness I affirm; His oneness I*
*confess, Who made of nothing earth and sky*
*and all that is within them through His love,*
*and rules creation from His throne above!*

And so I call my God as witness to
my soul, that all that I have said to you
in this confession is the truth; I do
not lie. Nor would I wish to write to you
to gain from you or to ingratiate
myself with you, or earn respect. Berate
me if you will; if my integrity
to you still is not clear, it is for me
1 Jn. 3.21 enough that I possess it in my heart.
Moreover, He Who calls and sets apart
unto Himself His faithful ones is true
1 Thess. 5.24 in what He promises. His Word will do
for me; He never lies.

For I can see
that even now the Lord exalted me,
though I unworthy am of this and of
the way He has provided in His love
for me. I know that I am better fit
for poverty and trouble than to sit
in luxury and wealth. Just so the Lord

2 Cor. 8.9 was poor for us, as it is in His Word
recorded. I am indigent and poor,
and even if I ever wanted more
than this, I do not have it. This is how
I estimate myself before Him now;
and daily I expect that I will be
betrayed or killed or put in slavery
again, or something of the kind. And yet,
because His Word is sure, I do not let
Ps. 27.1-3 such things deter or frighten me. For I
have thrown myself upon the Lord Most High,
Who reigns throughout the earth and sky, just as
1 Pt. 5.7 the prophet says, "On Him your burdens cast,
and all your cares; He will sustain you." So
to God, the faithful, I commend my soul,
2 Cor. 5.20 for I am His ambassador, in spite
of my obscurity, and I am right
to trust myself to Him alone. For He
accepts no person, but selected me
to do this work, to be the least of all
His servants, who upon His mercy call.

Because of this, for all that He bestowed
on me, and all the kindnesses He showed
me, I'll repay Him with my life, though there
is nothing I can say, no promise dare
hope to fulfill, unless He gives to me
Phil. 2.12, 13 the power to do it. Let the Savior see
into my inner being: For greatly I
Mk. 10.28, 29 desire that I might drink His cup and die
for Him, as others have who loved Him.

So
may God permit that all of those who know
His Name because of me, be never lost

to me. And though my testimony cost
my very life, I pray that He may give
me strength, for Him to persevere and live,
until my dying day. What's more, I pray
that, if I've known success in any way
as His disciple, I might die with all
the other servants who upon Him call,
whose blood was shed for Him, though I receive
no proper burial, and no one grieve
for me, and though my corpse be torn from limb
to limb by dogs or beasts or birds: For Him
I would a martyr be. For if this should
my way of dying be, I know I would
Job 19.25-27 possess my soul and body once again
when Christ our Savior comes to judge all men.
1 Thess. 4.13-18 For we shall rise in Him as with the sun
when He returns, when glory has begun
to shine around the sons and daughters of
the living God, and we shall in His love
forever live, co-heirs with Christ, remade
1 Jn. 3.1-3 according to His image Who has paid
our debt; and we will reign with Him, and through
and in Him ever more.

His purpose to
obey, the sun arises every day,
and yet its splendor is a passing ray
of brilliance. All who worship it will be
to grievous punishment subjected. We,
however, who the True Sun, Christ the Lord,
1 Tim. 6.20 adore, will never perish. All who guard
His teaching will abide forever, just
as Christ Himself. So likewise all who trust
in Him will with Him reign, Who reigns on high

with God the Father and the Spirit, by
the power of God.

Again and yet again
I would reiterate what I to men
proclaim in this my declaration: I
declare in truth and joy of heart, and by
the Name of God and all His angels, I
have never had a reason, save that by
the Gospel and its promises declared,
to come back to this people, whom I dared
to flee. And I implore all those who fear
the Lord, and who agree to read or hear
this document, that, when you read it, you
would not in any way attribute to
this ignorant man a single one of all
the things that have been done, or any call
or guidance that to me was given by
the will of God. Instead, believe that I
2 Cor. 4.7 have been a vessel of the Lord, and He
has wrought these works and shown His gifts to me.
This is the truthful testimony I
declare to all of you before I die.

*For to the Lord belongs salvation, and*
*salvation rests within the Lord's strong hand;*
*to Christ belongs salvation. May it, Lord*
*be ever ours, according to Your Word.*

# STUDY GUIDE

# Lesson 1

*A Time for Heroes*

In our day, when role models routinely disappoint and heroes are few and far between, we in the Christian community need to discover in our heritage men and women whom we can emulate, exemplary saints who can help us to gain a clearer and more compelling vision of the life of faith and to grow in our understanding of and conviction concerning the mission of the Church in the world. What Paul wrote about the believers in the Old Testament and their ability to encourage us and give us hope (Rom. 15.4) is in many ways true of the heroes of the faith throughout Church history

1. Most Christians will identify one or another Biblical figure as something of a hero, someone with whom we can identify or who serves as a role model for our faith. Do any such Biblical heroes come to mind? In what ways do you look up to them? What have you learned from them?

2. How about individuals from other areas of life? Do you have any heroes from history or contemporary life who serve to guide and encourage you in your life? In what ways?

____________________________________________________________________________________________________

3. In this study we're going to be looking at Patrick, the patron saint of Ireland. You may already know some things about Patrick, as he is familiar to many people. What can you say that you know about Patrick? Do you see in him any potential for serving as a hero for you?

4. One of the ways that heroes serve us is by encouraging us or providing an example for us in areas of life where we are weak or where we would like to see more growth in our lives. Can you think of any such areas in your life? Can you see how Patrick's example might be helpful in any of these areas?

5. From Patrick we can learn about gratitude to God, personal piety, zeal for evangelism, courage and conviction in the service of the Lord, and love for the unlovely. Do you sense that you might need to grow in any of these areas? Which?

# Lesson 2

*Introduction and Prologue, lines 1-44*

For Christians, Patrick's story is timeless; yet it seems especially relevant to the times in which we live, both because of the similarities between our world and the world of the late Roman Empire and pre-Christian Ireland, and our own need to recover a proper understanding of the mission of the Church. Read the Introduction and Prologue, together with the notes and supporting Scripture, then answer the questions that follow.

1. Looking at the Prologue, and drawing on whatever else you may know about these times, what similarities can you identify between the period of the late Roman Empire and pre-Christian Ireland and our own times? Considering how the Gospel advanced even in such difficult times, how should this encourage us about the work of the Gospel today?

_______________________________________________

_______________________________________________

_______________________________________________

_______________________________________________

_______________________________________________

2. In those days many people believed that the end of history was near and that the Lord would return soon to gather up His people and to judge the nations. How did Church leaders of that day respond to this belief? According to Scripture, is there any sense in which this should be our own outlook as well? Should this help to determine the kinds of ministries we sponsor in our churches? In what way?

3. There were Christians in Ireland before Palladius arrived. He helped to lay a foundation upon which Patrick would build in his day. Take a look at 1 Cor. 3.5-9. In what ways can you see this passage illustrated in the coming of Christianity to Ireland? How should this encourage us as we think about the work of evangelizing our own communities?

4. As we shall see, Patrick was in some ways an unlikely candidate to be used of God in bringing the Gospel to the Irish people. When we think about what is needed to win our own communities for Christ, what kinds of things generally come to mind? Why do you think that churches today are so little involved in trying to reach the lost in their communities?

5. Patrick is one of the great saints of Church history. As the Introduction points out, there is much we can learn from him. As you look forward to studying Patrick's burden, what goals would you like to set for yourself? In other words, how would you like this study to help you grow as a Christian? When this study is finished, what will help you to know that it has been worthwhile?

________________________________________

________________________________________

________________________________________

________________________________________

# LESSON 3

*A Most Uncultivated Man, lines 45-164*

Patrick would have been the first to say that he was hardly qualified for the work of evangelizing the Irish, primarily because of his lack of formal education. But what he lacked in formal training he made up for in zeal for God's Word and a heart for the lost. Read lines 45-164, together with the notes and supporting Scripture, then answer the questions below.

1. In his later years, Patrick felt compelled to set forth his burden in order to silent critics who had begun to question the validity of his ministry. Yet it is clear that Patrick's faith was orthodox and his ministry quite successful. What indications do you see here, early in his burden, that God had blessed Patrick's ministry among the Irish people? How might a missionary today, who had accomplished this much, describe his work to his supporters back home? Do you know any missionaries like this?

2. The heart of Patrick's preaching is revealed in lines 121-164. Let's examine this more closely. From what you read here, summarize Patrick's doctrine of the Trinity:

3. Patrick preached Jesus as Lord. What did that mean, and what do men owe to Him, and why?

4. What is necessary for men in order that they might know salvation from the Lord?

5. See if you can take Patrick's brief confession, as paraphrased in lines 121-164, and work it into a presentation of the Gospel that you might use with a neighbor or friend. Where would you start? How might you bring Scripture into your presentation? What must your friend know in order to be saved? Write out your brief presentation below:

# Lesson 4

*A Most Uncultivated Man, lines 165-282*

We hear many reasons why Christians are not actively involved in sharing their faith with their friends and neighbors. All of them are some variation on the idea that they do not feel qualified to do the work of an evangelist. Patrick felt some of that lack of qualification himself, but he did not let that keep him from doing what he knew the Lord had called him—and, indeed, every Christian—to do. Read lines 165-282, together with the notes and supporting Scripture, then answer the following:

1. What seems to have been the main reason that Patrick referred to himself as "a most uncultivated man"? How did his lack of cultivation show itself? How might you expect to hear someone today protest that he or she was not qualified to share the Gospel with others?

2. What caused Patrick to miss out on the formal education that his critics were able to enjoy? How did he see this as being in the plan of God for his life and ministry? Did Patrick believe that his lack of formal education disqualified him from serving as an evangelist? Why not?

______________________________________________

______________________________________________

______________________________________________

______________________________________________

3. Why did Patrick believe that, in spite of his lack of formal training, he needed to press on in following the Lord's call? What was driving him? How can you see that he believed God would use him in spite of his lack of cultivation?

______________________________________________

______________________________________________

______________________________________________

______________________________________________

4. To what does Patrick appeal as proof that he was only doing the Lord's will when he went to Ireland? How should his effectiveness in ministry, in spite of all his shortcomings, encourage us today in the work of reaching out to the lost?

______________________________________________

______________________________________________

______________________________________________

______________________________________________

5. What are some of the reasons you have heard why Christians today are not more active in sharing the Gospel? Recall Patrick's motivations in going among the Irish: gratitude to God for His grace, obedience to God's command, and love for the lost. How might a better grasp of these motives help in overcoming the reasons for not witnessing that you listed above?

# LESSON 5

*Holy Servant Boy, lines 283-467*

Patrick's captivity in Ireland marked the beginning of his service to the Lord, for it was in the loneliness of slavery that he turned to the God of his youth and began to learn how to depend on him. His experience shows us that God uses even our trials to fit us for service in His Kingdom. Read lines 283-467, together with the notes and supportive Scripture, then answer the questions that follow.

1. As Patrick looked back on his sufferings, what was his attitude toward the trials God had brought into his life? Do you think that was how he felt at the time he was carried away into slavery (lines 305-08)? How do you typically react to the trials, difficulties, and problems that God allows to come into your life?

_______________________________________________

_______________________________________________

_______________________________________________

_______________________________________________

_______________________________________________

2. Patrick "turned to prayer" in order to cope with his situation. How would you describe Patrick's practice of prayer at this time? How does your own practice of prayer compare to his? What did Patrick gain from his prayers? How can Patrick's experience of prayer encourage and instruct you?

___

___

___

___

3. Patrick was convinced that God spoke to him in dreams. In his *Confession* he cites eight different occasions when God revealed His will for him through a dream. Our tendency is to dismiss such accounts as either greatly exaggerated or simply untrue. But Patrick did not have the benefit of God's Word, and he had no teachers or counselors to guide him. Is it unreasonable to expect that God might "speak" to him through the medium of a dream? Why or why not? Have you ever had an experience where you felt as though God was "speaking" to you in some direct way like this? Given the fact that we do have God's Word to guide us, how should we evaluate such experiences in our own lives (Ps. 36.9)?

___

___

___

___

4. Twice during the period of his deliverance Patrick refused to submit to pagan rituals in order to please the people who were helping him. Do you ever experience pressure to conform to the practices of unbelievers around you? Can you give an example? How should Patrick's experience instruct us to respond at such times? What will this require of us? What might it cost us?

5. We could say that Patrick maintained a balance between a spoken and a lived witness before the sailors who delivered him. How can you see this? In what ways is this instructive for us? How can you see that God was using this time during his deliverance to further prepare him for his ministry later on? In what ways was he continuing to grow? How does Patrick's experience encourage us to regard the daily opportunities for witness that the Lord brings into our lives?

# LESSON 6

*Holy Servant Boy, lines 467-542*

God had been preparing Patrick for his life's calling ever since he was a child, but especially when He intervened to deliver him from slavery. The critical moment for Patrick came in a dream in which he felt the people of Ireland calling him back to labor among them. How does God's call come to us today? Read lines 467-542, together with the notes and supportive Scripture, then answer the following questions.

1. Patrick was no doubt much relieved to be back at home among friends and family again. Yet God had other plans for him. What kinds of temptations might have kept Patrick from responding to what he felt God was calling him to do? What kinds of temptations keep us from obeying the will of God for our lives?

________________________________________________
________________________________________________
________________________________________________
________________________________________________

2. Upon receiving the call to return to the place of his enslavement and serve the Lord, Patrick "was pierced by great emotion." What kinds of emotions do you think he must have felt? Why? According to line 519, what was the dominant emotion that Patrick felt? Why? How did God's preparation to this point help him to overcome this emotion? Do you think this emotion keeps people from following the Lord's leading in their lives today? Explain:

______________________________________________

______________________________________________

______________________________________________

______________________________________________

______________________________________________

______________________________________________

3. Patrick again shows how important prayer was in his life. How did he describe his prayers at this particular time (lines 523-541)? Have you ever experienced this? What was the result of this "wrestling" in prayer?

______________________________________________

______________________________________________

______________________________________________

______________________________________________

______________________________________________

______________________________________________

4. Patrick's experience gives us some insight into discerning the will of God for our own lives. He had a sense, received in a dream, of what God wanted him to do. How might Christians today gain a sense of God's calling in their lives? He wrestled in prayer and reflection on God's Word to help him overcome his fears, determine whether or not this was indeed God's leading for his life, and make the decision to obey. Reflecting on Patrick's experience, how might you counsel a young person trying to discern the Lord's leading in his or her life concerning a calling to ministry?

_______________________________________________

_______________________________________________

_______________________________________________

_______________________________________________

_______________________________________________

5. Look back at the goals you set for this study in lesson 2. Are you making any progress in realizing these goals? In what ways? If not, what do you think is keeping you from it? Are you finding any ways that you can identify in your own life with Patrick's experience of knowing the Lord and discerning His will?

_______________________________________________

_______________________________________________

_______________________________________________

_______________________________________________

_______________________________________________

# LESSON 7

*Kept Within His Grace, lines 543-700*

Patrick's preparation to follow the Lord's calling was not without adversity. There was much to learn, and he would have to overcome not a few obstacles before he would be appointed bishop over the Irish Christians. But his sense of calling from the Lord was so strong that it kept him focused and working hard to be ready for when the Lord would finally allow him to realize his vision. Read lines 543-700, together with the notes and supporting Scriptures, then answer the questions that follow.

1. Patrick appears to have gone to Ireland fairly shortly after having his vision confirmed by the Lord. His obedience to his call was immediate, although he would require many years of preparation before he would fully realize his vision. God has called all of us as servants in His Kingdom. To what kind service do you think the Lord might be calling you? What sorts of steps in preparation might that require?

________________________________________

________________________________________

________________________________________

2. Patrick had some hurdles to get over before he realized his vision. What were they? One in particular seems to have rankled him. How did he feel about this matter coming up at the time he was first suggested for the bishopric? Have you ever felt as though you were being unfairly judged, or that you were betrayed by a friend? How did your response compare with Patrick's on this occasion?

3. Patrick said that he found grace to sustain him during his preparation and trials through the Word of God (line 686). How can you see from the supporting Scriptures in this section that this was so? In what ways did the Word of God inform Patrick's outlook on life? To what extent does the Bible play that kind of role in your life?

4. Patrick seems to have found through his sense of calling, prayer, the Word of God, and a patient spirit the resources he needed to pursue and finally realize God's vision for his life. In a brief statement, summarize the role that each of these seems to have played during the period of Patrick's preparation for his calling:

5. In what ways can Patrick's example be helpful to you in discerning the Lord's leading in your life and preparing you for whatever calling He may have for you? How can his example help you in dealing with the various obstacles, trials, challenges, and hurdles that you will certainly face?

___

___

___

# LESSON 8

*Undertaking for the Lord, lines 705-862*

Undeterred by rejection, Patrick continued to prepare for, and actually to begin, his ministry among the Irish. In this section we begin to get a closer look at the ways God used him. Read lines 705-862, together with the notes and supporting Scriptures, then answer the questions that follow.

1. Patrick is at pains to convince his readers that everything he did was in obedience to the Lord's call and leading in his life. In what ways can you see this in this section?

______________________________________________

______________________________________________

______________________________________________

2. Do you think it was easy for Patrick to leave his home and go back to Ireland? What temptations faced him as he embarked on his calling? How did God sustain him? What temptations might you expect to encounter as you begin to follow the Lord's leading in your life? Following Patrick's example, how should you deal with those temptations?

______________________________________________

______________________________________________

______________________________________________

3. Summarize as much as you can of the ministry activities that Patrick pursued and of the results he achieved during his ministry. Whom did Patrick credit for his success?

---

---

---

4. How would you describe Patrick's understanding of the life of a disciple? To what are the followers of Christ called? What does this require of them? Is this an understanding of the life of faith that is grounded in Scripture? How well does Patrick's view of the life of a disciple describe you?

---

---

---

5. Patrick understood that "God is faithful to His Word" (lines 847-48). Which aspects of God's faithfulness was Patrick counting on for his ministry? Are these same promises held out to us? How can we learn to rely on God's promises more like Patrick did? How might we help one another?

---

---

---

# Lesson 9

*Undertaking for the Lord, lines 862-972*

Patrick continues to argue the blessing of the Lord on his ministry in defense against certain detractors who would like to see him recalled. Read lines 862-972, together with the notes and supporting Scripture, then answer the questions that follow.

1. The Celtic tradition retained important roles for women in the ministry of the Kingdom. Patrick introduces us to the calling of virgin (lines 862-892). Using your imagination, what must the life of a virgin of the Lord been like? What temptations might such women have faced in making and carrying out this decision? Can you think of any roles for women in the Church today that might be analogous to this? Explain:

______________________________________________

______________________________________________

______________________________________________

______________________________________________

2. Patrick determined not to go to Britain to answer the charges that were being laid against him. Instead, he offered his *Confession*, not to his critics primarily, but to the people he served, in order to justify both his work and his refusal to leave the field. What risks did Patrick run in taking this tack in response to his detractors? What temptations did he have to overcome in making this decision? Can we learn anything from him about how we ought to respond to unjust or unfounded charges that may be made against us?

3. Patrick confesses that, besides the temptations presented to him in the charges of his detractors, he was daily faced with temptations to betray the Lord and His work. Look carefully at lines 911-972. What kinds of temptations does he mention? How did Patrick deal with the various temptations he experienced in his ministry? What can we learn from him about resisting the devil in our own lives?

4. In lines 939-961 Patrick, reflecting again on his initial rejection for the episcopate, makes two admissions. What are they? What does this suggest about his initial response to his rejection? Time can sometimes help to put things into a more perfect perspective, even the trials that come our way, as Patrick seems to admit here. That being so, why does it make sense, when trials come, to give thanks to God (line 940) and to stay on task while we wait upon the Lord to do His good and perfect will in our lives, rather than, say, fall into depression, anxiety, or even anger?

5. Using his own example as a basis, Patrick interjects a mild rebuke to his colleagues in ministry (lines 968-970). What seems to be the intent of this rebuke? Is there any sound advice for us in this, for example, about listening to gossip concerning our friends and colleagues, about standing up for those whom we know to be solid servants of the Lord, etc.? How should we deal with such things when they come our way?

# LESSON 10

*A Man of Full Integrity, lines 973-1068*

In this section Patrick responds head-on to his critics. They were charging him with purely monetary motives in ministry and suggesting that he ought to be removed from the field because of this. Read lines 973-1068, together with the notes and supporting Scripture, then answer the following.

1. To what does Patrick initially appeal in his response to these charges (lines 981-985)? What was it that he expected his colleagues to have known about him on this basis? Would you have equal confidence making such an appeal to support your own claim to be a follower of Christ? Why or why not?

2. Patrick says he took specific steps throughout his ministry to protect himself against just the kind of charges that were being laid against him at this time. What steps did he take? Is there any advice for us in his example, not only in the area of financial integrity, but in other areas? Explain:

---

---

---

3. Patrick mentions two motivations for working hard at maintaining his integrity (lines 1006-1011). What were they? What do you learn about Patrick's heart from this? How can we today use such motivations to help us maintain our integrity, and why should we?

---

---

---

4. Rather than seeking to gain financially from his ministry, Patrick insists that he made many financial sacrifices on behalf of those he served. Can you point out the examples he offers? What kinds of sacrifices should we be willing to make on behalf of those we are called to serve, in whatever our area of service might be?

---

---

---

5. Patrick indicates that the work of the Kingdom requires a great deal of financial sacrifice on the part of those who are called to serve the Lord in this work (lines 1061-1068). This is true today as well. Consider what is involved in putting a missionary on the field. Who should be willing to bear the cost of such an undertaking? What should the role of the local church be in this? Of individual believers? Of the missionary? What can you do to promote more sacrificial giving on the part of Christian missions in your church?

# LESSON 11

*Bishop to the Irish People, lines 1069-1263*

In this and the next section we will be looking at Patrick's *Letter Against the Soldiers of Coroticus*, which he wrote in order to excommunicate certain villains who had attacked and carried off Christians into slavery. We will get a good look at the heart of Patrick in his concern for the honor of God and the well being of the people under his care. Read lines 1069-1263, together with the notes and supporting Scripture, then answer the questions below.

1. What was the problem provoking this angry outburst from Patrick? Do we see any similar problems confronting the Church of our Lord today? Can you discuss any of which you are aware?

____________________________________________
____________________________________________
____________________________________________
____________________________________________
____________________________________________

2. We can see Patrick trying to follow a decent and orderly attempt to redress this situation. What did he do first? How was that received? What threat to Patrick's ministry and the Church in Ireland did this response pose?

3. Patrick means to excommunicate Coroticus and his thugs. See if you can identify specific examples of his language indicating this. How were the other believers in Ireland supposed to respond to Patrick's decision? What can we learn from Patrick's treatment of unrepentant sinners about the practice of church discipline today?

4. How would you describe Patrick's attitude in this part of the *Letter Against the Soldiers of Coroticus*? Is it a proper attitude? Why or why not? Why kinds of situations might justify such an attitude on our parts?

5. Patrick sees the recalcitrance of Coroticus and his soldiers as a threat to his own ministry. In what way would this have been true? What does this suggest about the credibility of church leaders who knowingly tolerate sin in their congregations or organizations? What is required of individual believers in helping to keep themselves, their churches, and their ministries pure and unblemished before the Lord?

# Lesson 12

*Bishop to the Irish People, lines 1263-1384*

We conclude our look at Patrick's *Letter Against the Soldiers of Coroticus*. We will see some additional aspects of Patrick's pastoral heart and try to apply them to our own situations in the Church today. Read lines 1263-1384, together with the notes and supporting Scriptures, then answer the questions that follow.

1. How can you see in this section that Patrick is a man of the Church, that is, that he determined to follow established procedures in how he responded to this crisis? What was that meant to suggest to the soldiers of Coroticus? To the people under Patrick's care? How should it counsel us today?

2. Describe Patrick's attitude toward those who had been slain or carried off into slavery. Knowing that there are Christians suffering for their faith all over the world today, how should Patrick's example instruct us? What is our responsibility for our suffering brethren in Christ?

3. In the midst of this tragedy Patrick was able to find some solace. In what did his comfort lie? What does this suggest about Patrick's vision of life? What can we learn from him about keeping our eyes on the Lord in the midst of trials and difficulties?

4. How did Patrick try to enlist the aid of the believing community in rescuing the suffering brethren? What would that have required on the part of those believers who chose to follow his instructions? What would they have risked to do so?

5. Review the reading and your responses for these last two lessons. Using this material as your guide, lay out a strategy for enlisting your church in beginning to take more interest in the plight of suffering Christians around the world today:

# Lesson 13

*His Ambassador, lines 1385-1498*

We bring our study of the burden of Patrick to a close. Perhaps nowhere in his writings more than in this passionate peroration do we see into the heart of a true man of God. Read lines 1385-1498, together with the supporting Scripture, then answer the questions below.

1. How can you see that, regardless of the opinions or judgments of men, Patrick was content to rest on the Lord and his own sense of God's leading in his life? How might such a conviction serve you in your walk with the Lord?

2. How can you see that, in the face of constant danger and depravation, Patrick was resolved to trust in the Lord to care for him? What can you learn from his example about trusting the Lord for your daily needs?

3. How would you describe Patrick's attitude toward his earthly life? What did it mean? For what was it to be used? How might one expect to make the most of his time on earth?

4. What have you learned from the burden of Patrick in each of the following areas?

Gratitude to God

Personal piety

Evangelistic zeal

Courage and conviction

Loving the unlovely

5. Review the goals for this study that you set for yourself in lesson 2. To what extent, and in what specific ways, have you been able to realize those goals?

90000
9 780738 835365